Toxic Stress

7 Steps to Recovery

Toxic Stress

7 Steps to Recovery

Marilyn J. Varcoe, Ph.D.,
and Patricia Burnett

ANN ARBOR
MEDIA GROUP

Toxic Stress: 7 Steps to Recovery
by Marilyn Varcoe, Ph.D., and Patricia Burnett

Published by J. W. Edwards, Inc., by special arrangement with
The Ann Arbor Media Group LLC
2500 S. State Street
Ann Arbor, Michigan 48104

ISBN 1-930842-02-3

Jacket design by Andrea Worthing
Jacket and chapter opening illustrations by V. Weiss, M.D.,
    Biomedical Illustrator, www.valerieweiss.com.
Profile images by Deb Geno, M.A.

Printed and bound by Edwards Brothers, Inc., Ann Arbor, Michigan.

08 07 06 05 04   10 9 8 7 6 5 4 3 2 1

The patient stories in this book are true and come from more than twenty-five years of Dr. Varcoe's practice in Pennsylvania and Florida. Names and other details have been changed to disguise identities in compliance with ethical practices and federal patient privacy laws.

We dedicate this book to our mothers,
Mary Hudasko and Rosemary Johnson,
who taught us to live gracefully, appreciate our blessings
and share our strength.

Contents

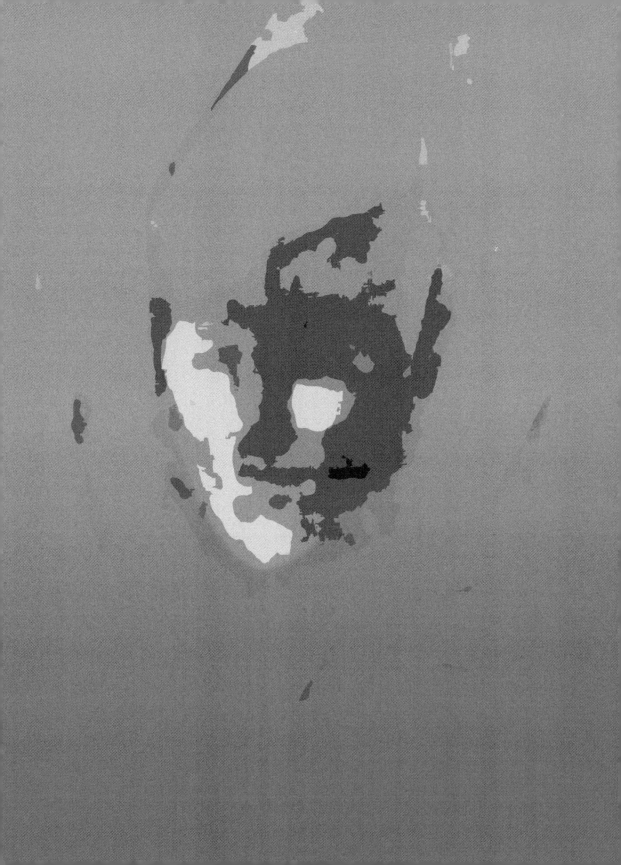

Introduction

In my practice as a psychologist in Naples, Florida, I see many patients who suffer from "toxic stress." By my definition, toxic stress is a difficult life situation compounded by three additional factors: physical damage or illness, depression and anxiety.

Toxic stress is living with an abusive husband or wife, having high blood pressure, feeling hopeless and anxious about your future.

Toxic stress is hating the politics of your workplace, catching every cold that comes along, withdrawing from friends and flashing back to a mugging.

Toxic stress is declaring bankruptcy, having diabetes, not sleeping and having panic attacks.

What I see most often in my practice is a person living with ongoing stress—a difficult life situation—who becomes ill and winds up in a physician's office. Often it is the physical illness or damage that becomes the wake-up call. When someone cannot function in the day-to-day world because of physical symptoms, he or she sees a doctor. Maybe it is a heart condition or severe gastric problems or migraines. Research shows irrefutably that stress-induced hormones, especially one called cortisol, weaken the immune system and increase susceptibility to many illnesses and medical conditions. The physician asks questions and concludes that stress contributed to the medical condition and that the patient's inability to handle the stressors has caused some level of depression and anxiety.

The doctor knows that the patient's physical and mental health is seriously jeopardized until he or she diminishes the stress or at least controls the detrimental effects of stress, and that is when the doctor refers the patient to me. When your life is out of control, that is also when you buy a self-help book. Or if the warning signs are flashing, now is the time to change your future. Prevention could save your life.

Controlling the harmful effects of stress is basic stress management. This book provides that but goes beyond stress management to include strategies to overcome the rest of the toxic stress matrix, including depression and anxiety in many forms.

These approaches can be supplemented with psychotherapy and medications, or be purely self-help, depending on your degree of impairment. This book also encourages using cognitive strategies and techniques—changing how you think about your life and yourself. You will hear how many of my patients gained self-insights and problem-solved their way out of very difficult life situations. Further, this book encourages wellness approaches such as stress-busting diet, exercise and other alternatives for coping with stress. For example, stress eating is a very real problem for many people, and I can help you overcome the emotional and physiological urges to overdo, overeat and indulge in substances that only exacerbate the stressors.

I can offer you hope. My approach with new patients is to give them hope that they will once again function in the day-to-day world and experience health and happiness. I often offer them a time frame by which they can expect to feel better. Sitting in my office, pouring out their stories, they cannot see that happy ending. When toxic stress is swirling stress hormones through their bodies, when depression and anxiety have shut off any problem-solving ability, I have to persuade them to look for the light at the end of the tunnel.

My practice and this book draw primarily upon the research-proven concepts and techniques of cognitive behavioral psychology. When you say "psychology," many people conjure Freud and a patient on a couch telling about his childhood and the unconscious. While the past undoubtedly affects the present, in cognitive behavioral psychology, the emphasis is less on the distant past and more on solving an immediate problem. "Cognitive" means how you think. Cognitive behavioral psychology presumes that if you change the way you think about something, you can change the way you feel and behave about it. You can harness your brain in new ways so that you can feel better and problem-solve more effectively.

While this is a self-help book, if you truly cannot function at work or at home, you need professional help, and perhaps medication. Call your regular doctor for an appointment and a referral.

In this book you will read the stories of more than fifty patients who have experienced toxic stress—the dangerous melding of a difficult life situation, physical damage, depression and anxiety. Almost every patient profiled here as having toxic stress also had a family history of mental disorder or past personal trauma affecting mental health. Genetic predisposition and family environment are strong predictors of mental health problems and of vulnerability to stress, depression and anxiety. Many of these patients were in far greater trouble than you probably are, and, yet, all of them improved and went on to happier, less stressful, more healthful lives. They are your proof that toxic stress is treatable.

From more than twenty-five years as a practicing psychologist, seeing thousands of patients with toxic stress, I am sharing with you 7 Steps to Recovery from Toxic Stress.

The 7 Steps are:

1. Understand stress and the mind-body connection
2. Dig out of depression
3. Defeat anxiety and anger
4. Think with the "bright side" of your brain
5. Love and be loved
6. Commit to health and wellness
7. Take charge and create order

I will share proven techniques and how they worked for my patients. At the end of each chapter, you may select strategies and techniques to help you toward your recovery. Step by step, you will flow through the book, ending with a selection of strategies and techniques that becomes your own 7-Step Action Plan to Recovery. Changing your life is never easy, but your 7-Step Action Plan can help you get off to a great start today!

Dr. Marilyn J. Varcoe

Step 1

Understand Stress and the Mind-Body Connection

It is the mind that makes the body.
—Sojourner Truth (1797?–1883) U.S. abolitionist, reformer

Step 1

Understand Stress and the Mind-Body Connection

Jillian's Toxic Stress

My patient "Jillian" had terminal pancreatic cancer. Despite surgeries, chemotherapy and other aggressive medical treatment, she had only three months to live. Her doctor referred her to me because she was angry over her fate. Anger equates to stress, physiologically triggering the same kinds of effects, symptoms and vulnerabilities. Quickly, I recognized the matrix of toxic stress in her life.

Working together, we determined that Jillian's anger went much deeper than her end-of-life reality. She was most angry with her son, a textbook "bad boy" in his thirties, whom she blamed, rightly or wrongly, for her illness. Though pancreatic cancer is one of the least treatable forms of cancer, I confirmed for her that chronic, unrelieved stress weakens the immune system and heightens vulnerability to many diseases and life-threatening conditions, including some cancers. Jillian's doctor had told me, too, that heavy drinking had contributed to liver and pancreas damage.

The renegade son—so much like his father—had ruthlessly stolen the family business from her after her husband's death. Jillian had suffered indignity as well as financial loss while still grieving over her husband.

When the primary source of her anger came to light, however, Jillian said to me, "Before I die I have to put my life in order, and I have to forgive my son."

We worked through her anger to identify what he had put the family through, and when she was ready to talk, she called him. He flew in from the Midwest to meet with her in my office, with me present.

Jillian told him how betrayed she felt. He talked. She talked. And there were many tears. Ultimately, she forgave him, and he forgave her, his mother who was to die in less than three months.

Defying the odds of pancreatic cancer, however, Jillian lived another two years and credited her interim health to the removal of stress and anger from her life. In addition to her sessions with me and with her son, Jillian used relaxation techniques and visualization that I share later in this book. I also used hypnosis in her treatment.

Jillian's story is the most dramatic example of the mind-body connection from my practice, but the mind-body connection is the central component of cognitive psychology and essential for anyone with toxic stress to embrace and use.

JILLIAN'S TOXIC STRESS

DIFFICULT LIFE SITUATION: Losing her husband and family business; financial instability, and then facing death with unresolved anger

PHYSICAL DAMAGE: Pancreatic cancer, damaged liver

DEPRESSION: Major depressive episode over her fate, hopelessness and grief

ANXIETY: Angry with her son; anxious about her illness and prognosis

ACTION PLAN: Psychotherapy, cognitive restructuring, relaxation exercises, hypnosis, visualization, confrontation/mediation with her son (See the Appendix for specific techniques and page numbers.)

MEDICATION: Zoloft® (antidepressant), BuSpar® (antianxiety)

For more than twenty-five years I have presented workshops on stress to service clubs, police officers, cruise ship passengers, physicians and other health care professionals and employee groups. I always start with statistics and research to build believers in my audience. There are no data expressly on toxic stress, but there is a wealth of statistics on stress and illness, on stress and depression and on stress and anxiety—the components of toxic stress.

Stress causes or contributes to 80 to 85 percent of all human illness and disease, physiological and psychological. I want you to know, this is not hyperbole. This is reality reported by the American Medical Association.

Stress is rampant.
- Stress sends us to the doctor. The American Institute of Stress estimates that 90 percent of all visits to doctors are stress-related, an even higher estimate than the American Medical Society's.
- More than half of all American adults report experiencing high levels of stress daily. (CNN poll)
- 75 percent of American adults report having "great stress" one day a week, and one out of every three say more than twice a week. (*Prevention* magazine poll)
- Every week 95 million Americans take some type of medication for some kind of stress-related condition.

Stress plays a role in coronary disease, the leading cause of death in America.
- Stress can cause sudden cardiac arrest, which is a usually fatal disruption of the heart's electrical signals. Women are more vulnerable to stress-induced attacks than men. (University of Minnesota clinical research)
- For people who already have heart disease stress is as deadly a factor as smoking or high cholesterol. (University of Florida College of Medicine clinical research)
- Mental stress can reduce blood flow to the heart and increase the risk of death in people with coronary artery disease. (University of Florida Health Sciences Center clinical research)
- Stress in the form of grief increases the odds of a heart attack 14-fold in the 24 hours following the death of a loved one.
- Stress in the form of anger more than doubles the likelihood of heart attack in the two-hour period after someone experiences intense anger.
- Stress increases the risk of stroke. Among middle-aged white men, a study showed that when stress elevated blood pressure, the risk of stroke increased by 72 percent over men whose blood pressure did not rise when under stress. (University of Michigan)

Cancers
- Stress raises the risk of prostate cancer. The risk of having an abnormal PSA, the predictor of prostate cancer, is three times as great for men living with stress as without. (State University of New York, Stony Brook)
- Stress weakens the immune system and the mind-body ability to defend against existing disease, such as breast cancer. (Ohio State University)

Muscles and spine damage
- Stress increases the risk of back injury, the most prevalent and costly kind of on-the-job injury. One theory is that workers tense up before lifting, or are distracted by their thoughts. (Ohio State University)

Gastrointestinal ailments
- Stress increases the vulnerability to stomach ulcers. Though research has established that most ulcers stem from a specific bacteria, people under stress are more likely to have ulcers. (Harvard Medical School)
- Stress triggers diarrhea, nausea, constipation, stomach cramps and other gastrointestinal conditions in many people. (Harvard Medical School)

Colds and upper-respiratory illness
- People living with high stress are 1.7 times more likely to get a cold than people living with low stress. In one study, people under stress contracted 2.7 upper respiratory infections in a six-month period, compared to 1.5 illnesses for people with low stress. Stress weakens the immune system.

Psychological disorders
- Half of all people with depression also suffer from stress. Eighty-five percent of people with depression suffer from anxiety, as well.

The gender gap
- Stress adversely affects women more than men, possibly because women juggle more home and work duties and experience guilt or anxiety over these situations. (Harvard Medical School)

- Women create their own additional stress with self-expectations to have a good relationship, be happy, be well liked, maintain the house, achieve on the job and—very important—be thin. Women link their self-esteem to their appearance, especially their weight. (Harvard Medical School)

Stress is also expensive.

- Job stress costs American business and industry an estimated $150 billion a year in absenteeism, accidents and turnover. (National Institute for Occupational Safety and Health)

Richard M. Suinn of Colorado State University, and a past president of the American Psychological Association, reviewed a vast library of medical research on stress and found "clear confirmatory evidence that stress expressed as anxiety and anger is indeed hazardous to health."

In a finding reported to an annual meeting of the American Psychological Association, Suinn said, "Over the years, anxiety and hostility have been consistently demonstrated to increase vulnerability to illness, impair the immune system, increase levels of cholesterol, prevent adjustment to chronic pain, increase risk of atherosclerosis, and even increase mortality from both cardiovascular disease and all causes."

These are the statistics and the research behind them that demonstrate that toxic stress, as I define it, is not just debilitating but truly life-threatening.

Do you suffer from toxic stress? Begin your own self-diagnosis here.

TOXIC STRESS SELF-SCREENING

Identify My Stressors

Check each one that applies to me during the past six months.
Add the checks for my total score below.

Relationship Stressors

_____ Death of a loved one

_____ Separation or divorce from spouse or significant other

_____ Domestic abuse incident

_____ Recent marriage or cohabitation

_____ Sexual dissatisfaction with partner

_____ Relationship break-up

_____ Marital or relationship discord

_____ Spouse/significant other having affair

_____ Fighting with in-laws

_____ Conflicting values over parenting, child discipline

_____ Step-parenting conflicts

_____ Single-parenting issues

_____ Conflict with former spouse or significant other

_____ Dysfunctional family

_____ Parenting difficult children

_____ Violent or law-breaking child

_____ A child leaving home

_____ Caregiving pressures of aged parent or spouse

_____ Sexual abuse episode

_____ Loss of a significant friendship

_____ Jealousy experiences toward partner

_____ Spouse/significant other doesn't contribute fair share of the household chores

_____ Early childhood trauma, such as abuse or death of a parent

_____ Living or working with someone who abuses alcohol or drugs

Total possible: 24 My score _____

Financial Issues

_____ Bankruptcy

_____ Foreclosure

_____ Credit-card indebtedness

_____ Collection agency threats

_____ Conflicting values in family about spending, saving money

_____ Decrease in income

_____ Loan repayment pressure

_____ Financial losses

_____ Tax problems

_____ Unprepared for retirement

_____ Medically uninsured

_____ Pressing legal problems

Total possible: 12 My score _____

Health Issues

____ Recent diagnosis of serious medical conditions

____ Ongoing chronic or acute medical problems

____ Recent surgery

____ Accident victim

____ Chronic pain

____ Chronic fatigue

____ Caring for sick spouse or child

____ Infertility

____ Impotence or other sexual dysfunction

____ Weight gain or loss

____ Physical disability

____ Inability to relax

____ Lack of exercise

____ Loss of sight or hearing

Total possible: 14 My score ____

Mental Health Issues

____ Depression symptoms

____ Chronic anxiety

____ Frequent panic attacks

____ Phobias

____ Sleep disorders

____ Memory/concentration problems

____ Bipolar

____ Alcohol/drug abuse

____ Persistent procrastination

____ Disabling perfectionism

____ Recent traumatizing incident

____ Other diagnosed mental disorder

Total possible: 12 My score ____

Work Life Stressors

____ Recent job loss, demotion or firing

____ Recent career change

____ Chronic unemployment

____ Job searching problems

____ Job performance pressures

____ Job dissatisfaction

____ Long work hours

____ Irregular shift work

____ More than one job

____ Job danger

____ Long commute

____ Child care complications

____ Work absences

____ Dissatisfaction with work environment

____ Computer or other technology frustrations

____ Customer demands

____ Bad boss

____ Recent retirement

Total possible: 18 My score ____

Other External Stressors

____ Crime victim

____ Holiday pressures

____ Unsafe housing or neighborhood

____ Planning a wedding or other
   major event

____ Death of a pet

____ Car or transportation problems

Total possible: 6 My score ____

Grand total possible: 86 My score ____

Most of these issues, circumstances and conditions equate to the Difficult Life Situations that are a core element of Toxic Stress. Therefore, any one could be sufficient to disrupt your life and generate a barrage of hormones affecting your immune system and health. It is instructive, however, to see just how many stressors coexist. You gain a better picture of why your life is out of control.

While this self-screening is instructive, it is not the scientifically proven test used by many professionals. The Holmes-Rahe Life Readjustment Scale is re-search-based, and you may want to score yourself on it, as well. It is widely available on the Internet. Do a search for Holmes-Rahe. The downside to that test is that it is based on stressors as they existed in the 1950s, and we know that today is a different world.

One basic fact about stress is that it is cumulative. "Good" stress such as a job promotion is added to "bad" stress such as a divorce, and the result is still too many stress hormones attacking your health. That is why it is especially important to deeply analyze your life and identify stressors. You comprehend how great the damage can be.

People sometimes say, "I'm over the top of the stress scale." Anyone with toxic stress is over the top of the stress scale, and it may be because one really awful life situation imposed itself or because two or three difficult situations occurred and things went downhill from there.

What sets off stress for you may be different from what sends your best friend into butterflies and an aching neck. The contrast of Times Square on a Saturday night versus the everybody-knows-you of small town America provides a classic example of how one person's comfort zone can be another's stressor.

Each of us must identify the persons, places or things that personally trigger stress for us. In analyzing your own, you may find categorizing sources as "external" or "internal" to be helpful.

SELF-DIAGNOSIS

My Difficult Life Situation

Assess each area for stressors in my life and summarize them into my Difficult Life Situation, one of the four components of toxic stress.

External Stressors

My Environment: Noise, traffic, congestion, weather, living conditions...

My Relationships: With my boss, coworker, customer, spouse, children, relatives...

My Commitments and Requirements: Productivity, activities, deadlines, goals...

Internal Stressors

Low self-esteem	Preexisting depression
Perfectionism	Heredity and health
Unnecessary or undue self-pressure	Addictions
Impossible goals	Physical or sexual abuse as a child
Preexisting anxiety	Negative self-talk
Preexisting anger	

My Stressors

1. _____

2. _____

3. _____

4. _____

5. _____

6. _____

My Difficult Life Situation

_____

_____

_____

_____

My patient "Estela" had both external and internal stressors at work in her life, and she felt overwhelmed, inadequate, depressed and anxious.

Estela's Toxic Stress

Estela was a 23-year-old mother of hyperactive boys, ages two and five. She worked as a dental assistant, a job that paid just ten dollars an hour. Her husband worked two jobs to make ends meet, and to avoid a tense home life. Tight finances and difficult children finally got to him. He lashed out at Estela, verbally and physically, and then left to live with another woman.

Suddenly, Estela had all the responsibility, and her income barely covered day care. She worked two jobs and came home to unruly children. Emotionally, she felt like a zombie. "It's the stress," Estela said. "I cannot handle it anymore."

ESTELA'S TOXIC STRESS

DIFFICULT LIFE SITUATION: Dysfunctional family; workaholic husband left her; she had to work two jobs; and she had no support system

PHYSICAL DAMAGE: Colds, flu, gynecological trouble, migraine headaches

DEPRESSION: Severe depressive episode; she couldn't get out of bed to take care of the children, escaped into sleep; a general sadness, denial of her problematic situation

ANXIETY: About her dire circumstances, her future and her inability to cope

ACTION PLAN: Psychotherapy, time "off" from the children, problem-solving on time-management and financial issues, medications; behavioral management techniques for her children.

MEDICATION: Paxil CR™ (antidepressant), Xanax® (antianxiety)

Problem-Solving for Estela

Estela's problems were not easily solved. But once she understood what was happening to her physically and emotionally—and why—she could begin the problem-solving process. She was so caught up in the demands of two jobs and two difficult children that she could not see a way out, or believe that one might exist. Her instinct was to put the children first. But it was Estela herself who needed the greatest changes. She needed to give herself a break from all that responsibility, to have a few hours or an occasional day "off" so her body could rest from the onslaught of stress hormones. When she was more rested, the children were calmer. Helping Estela diminish the stress in life became detective work, sleuthing out what options for relief might be out there. Here is what she found.

Medications helped. Estela did not want to take an antidepressant, but she realized that she needed to be more aggressive in changing her life circumstances. With medications, she physically got more energy and the optimism she needed to begin to problem-solve and take more control of her life. She also could deal better with her ex-husband, and he agreed to take the boys one or two weekends a month. The boys had missed him and they were much happier. Reconnecting, the father also began paying child support, which allowed Estela to quit one of her jobs.

When the children were away, Estela allowed herself occasional weekends with a girlfriend in a nearby town. She even reconnected with her immediate family. She had been embarrassed to tell them of her problems. They offered her loving support, and when she was tired and burned out, she could visit for a weekend with them. She slept, rested and her parents cared for the children.

Estela participated in psychotherapy with me more enthusiastically until she felt strong enough to continue on her own and practice the skills she had learned in our sessions. Estela saw that taking control of her life and engaging in some personal pleasures gave her hope for a better future. We happily ended our sessions when her self-esteem had improved and she felt more positive about everything, even to the point of beginning to date and go out with friends.

More Perspective

Stress has a cause-effect-cause-effect dynamic. Stressors—including the difficult life situations that are central to toxic stress—come along every day, big and small. You think about them, then you feel them, then you react. Cause-effect-cause-effect. Your analysis and perception of your stressors affect your ability to adapt.

You evaluate your experience with the stressor. ("I can handle this," or "I cannot handle this.") Your perceptions determine how you feel about the stressor. ("I'm confident," or "I'm helpless.") Then your brain kicks in with what it considers the appropriate chemical response (more about that later) and you experience immediate physiological symptoms. If you are prepared to deal with the stressor, your brain sends out a little "rush" of hormones that feels like "energy" or "excitement." If you are less confident or fearful, your brain sends out more of the stress hormones and you experience symptoms that are more individualized and debilitating. Your heart pounds, you are short of breath. Some people get a tightness in their chest, muscle or back ache, lightheadedness, headache or digestive problems. There is an array of potential immediate physiological symptoms that people under great stress commonly experience.

As high stress continues, what you feel can grow more complex. Anxiety, anger and depression enter the picture, the building blocks of toxic stress. These responses, of course, have devastating effects on a person's dealings with other people, from family to coworkers to the guy who is tailgating you on the freeway. The damage accumulates and your body is more prone to acquire disease.

How Stress Affects Your Health

Here, again, is why toxic stress is such a serious health issue. When the brain comprehends the change or challenge you must make, it moves into the "alarm" stage. It's where cave man faced the saber-tooth tiger and had to choose fight or flight—put your life on the line or get out of there. In contemporary times when we are talking about stress, it is usually life-threatening in a more indirect, or at least, longer-term way. In the "alarm stage" the stress hormone cortisol is released into your body, causing your heart rate and breathing rate to speed up. Epinephrine and norepinephrine go out, too. Epinephrine is what we usually call adrenaline. Think about times you have "felt the adrenaline." Sometimes we say "adrenaline rush" because the hormone is speeding up the heart rate, and it really feels faster. It is actually adrenaline, norepinephrine and cortisol that cause the changes. A little can be good. Too much can be very damaging.

In the second stage of stress, the resistance stage, the body adapts or resists the stressor and the body regains its hormonal balance. The problem is, some people do not succeed. Unlike the cave man, whose stress was short-lived because he survived the encounter with the tiger, or he didn't, people today cannot slay the stressor so quickly. It may reappear repeatedly. We report to work every day. Dealing with our debts or difficult family members or international terrorism or a busy work schedule is continuous and ongoing. Unfortunately, our bodies have not developed an automatic off switch for the flood of hormones responding to the modern, extended version of the alarm state. Extended time in the alarm stage or the resistance stage means the body cannot repair itself, and eventually it becomes exhausted and even more vulnerable to illness. This is what the researchers theorize happens to people who are especially vulnerable to stress, such as women who were abused as children. They produce more hormones, even during mild stress.

A landmark study from Emory University found that women who were abused physically or sexually as children produce higher than normal levels of harmful stress hormones and show more persistent heart rate responses (indicative of anxiety) when experiencing stress. Women abused as children, who also had depression, produced six times more stress hormones than the norm. Researchers concluded that early childhood trauma changes brain chemistry, leaving a person long-term, and possibly permanently, more sensitive to stress, to anxiety and mood disorders, such as depression. These are three of four elements of toxic stress.

We are still learning how women may be affected by stress differently than men. The early research was based on all male subjects. But when the National Institutes of Health mandated in 1994 that government-funded research has to study effects on both genders, where appropriate, we began to get new insight.

In stress management, the goal is to get the body to send out less of these hormones, cut them off and arrive happily in the resistance stage, which is sometimes called "homeostasis" or "allostasis." This is a zone of biological factors in which the body functions efficiently and comfortably, and we feel at peace. We need this restful state in order to rejuvenate our body.

Stages of Toxic Stress

In the 1930s researcher Hans Selye, regarded as the "father of stress," developed the concept of stress, which he defined as the non-specific response of the body

Progression of Toxic Stress

Stages	Body Chemistry Changes	Mind & Body Changes
STRESSOR DIFFICULT LIFE SITUATION	HYPOTHALAMUS releases CRF which causes . . . PITUITARY to release ACTH which causes . . .	The brain recognizes danger.
ALARM STAGE	ADRENAL GLANDS to produce and release Adrenaline Cortisol DHEA NERVE CELLS to release norepinephrine	Heart rate rises Breathing quickens Energy increases Senses sharpen
RESISTANCE STAGE	Which causes . . . a balancing act of the hormones so cortisol levels do not go too high or too low, unless . . .	The stressor is conquered and the body returns to normal, unless . . .
EXHAUSTION	The balancing act fails and cortisol levels rise and remain high.	The stressor is not conquered and stress continues. Emotion, memory and behavior can be affected.
DEPRESSION	Brain chemistry can change; even the structure of brain cells can change.	Symptoms include unrelentinging sadness, lethargy, insomnia, loss of appetite.
ANXIETY	Neurotransmitters are depleted.	Symptoms include fearfulness, chronic worry, and panic.
PHYSICAL DAMAGE	The immune system is weakened and the body is vulnerable to disease.	Physical diseases can develop.

to any demands made upon it. He said stress has three "states"—the Alarm State in which the stressor threatens, the Resistance State in which you resist or adapt, and the Exhaustion State, where you wind up if you cannot stop the stressors, and the body systems begin to break down. Think of an inverted u-shaped curve. At the outset of stress, performance is enhanced, rising on the curve, as the mind and body react. But if the threat or change confronting you persists, then your performance and mental and physical health deteriorate, and the downward slide begins.

Toxic stress progresses similarly but acknowledges the breakdown of the brain chemistry, and depression and anxiety become symptomatic.

Alarm Stage: A stressor sets off your fight or flight mode. Your brain signals the adrenal glands, which increase the stress hormones cortisol and adrenaline. Muscles tense, the heart beats faster, your breathing quickens. Your body and your mind react in proportion to your perception of how difficult adapting to the stressor and impending change will be for you. These physiological changes early on generally enhance your performance—give you energy to resolve a threat.

Example: Your boss yells at you for failing to update the company web page with current sales information. Your mind races. Am I being fired? Where would I get another job? How can I survive? You are analyzing and problem-solving at a fast pace.

Resistance Stage: You handle the stressor. If you succeed, your body and mind return to their resting state. This is called homeostasis, a biologically safe zone in which the body functions efficiently and comfortably.

Example: You explain that a customer required immediate attention that took you away from your updating duties. The boss cools down. Things settle back to "normal."

Exhaustion: If, however, you do not handle your stressor, you enter the exhaustion stage. With no relief from the stress-incited hormones and the physical and mental damage, you are unable to function satisfactorily at home and in the workplace. Your body has exhausted its healthier options. The immune system weakens, and the body is susceptible to disease and dysfunction. Medical problems arise or worsen. Depression and/or anxiety take over.

Example: If someone in the office gets a cold, you get it next. Food just doesn't settle well. You develop acid reflux. You lose the pleasure of food, cannot sleep and lack any joy in your life.

Depression: The inability to overcome stressors and the continuing barrage of physical damage of extended, unrelieved stress can push a person into mild depression, or more serious depression requiring medical treatment and psychotherapy.

Example: You feel you are in limbo, where you cannot escape the pressure. You cannot see a way out of your problem. You begin to feel numb in interactions with others. Suddenly, all you want to do is sleep, or you cannot sleep at all. You avoid other people. You are constantly fatigued and irritable and out of control of your life.

Anxiety: Extended, unrelieved stress equates with anxiety, a medical condition characterized by an ongoing sense of dread and fear of real or imagined danger.

Example: You cannot kick the fear that something bad is about to happen. You read ominous signs into your boss's body language and every comment. You fear that something awful will happen and you will be unable to control it.

Cortisol, The Stress Hormone

The big chemical name in stress is cortisol. Cortisol is a hormone made in the adrenal glands, which are near the kidneys. When a stress cycles begins, cortisol secretion increases and sets off a series of physiological changes that ensure that the brain gets glucose for energy needed to deal with the stressor. Cortisol actually enters at the cell level, affects the nucleus and alters the type of proteins it produces.

Cortisol has such a huge effect on the body during time of stress that some physiologists define stress as an event that elicits increased levels of cortisol.

Medical researchers at Emory University are conducting follow-up studies to the landmark study that showed how early childhood trauma could change brain chemistry and leave persons more vulnerable to stress, as well as depression. They are evaluating the effectiveness of certain antidepressant medications that would block the action of CRF, an amino acid–containing peptide that is an early link in the brain chemistry cycle that eventually causes the overproduction of cortisol. The researchers believe that if they can do that, they could not only treat but possibly prevent adult psychiatric disorders related to early-life stress. This would be a major breakthrough in psychiatric medicine.

Here's a more detailed look at the chain of events in your body's reaction to stress, which is the difficult life situation in the toxic stress matrix.

THE CYCLE OF STRESS

1. The brain alerts the body that a stressor threatens you.
2. Nerve cells in the hypothalamus region of the brain release corticotrophin-releasing factor (CRF) into the blood stream that carries it to the anterior pituitary.
3. In response to CRF, the anterior pituitary releases adrenocorticotrophic hormone (ACTH) into the blood.
4. ACTH is transported to the adrenal gland and stimulates the production of cortisol in the adrenal cortex.
5. Cortisol courses through the blood stream.
6. Cortisol is transported back to the brain where it reduces further ACTH release and therefore the further production of too much cortisol.
7. Also in the stress progression DHEA (dihydroepiandosterone) is increased. This hormone buffers the body against detrimental effects of cortisol.
8. When stress is prolonged, DHEA levels fall and CRF remains raised. The hippocampus, another region of the brain involved with emotion, memory and behavior, can be affected.
9. Prolonged stress can bring about changes in basic brain chemistry, even altering the structure of brain cells.
10. The immune system is weakened by these changes.

Self-Diagnosis of Toxic Stress

Are you a victim of toxic stress? Check any conditions or diseases that you currently or periodically experience. In the second section identify other physical symptoms. Together, these equate to the "physical damage" component of toxic stress. To what degree and how often do you experience these symptoms? Are they a continuous health hazard for you?

SELF-DIAGNOSIS
Stress-Related Diseases and Conditions
(Check all that apply to me)

_____ Cardiovascular disease—including coronary artery disease, cerebral stroke, angina pectoris, cardiac arrhythmias and hypertension

_____ Cancer—including prostate cancer and breast cancer

_____ Ulcers

_____ Viral infections—including the common cold

_____ Muscular conditions—including tension headaches and head, back and neck aches

_____ Upper respiratory conditions—including asthma, allergies and hay fever

_____ Digestive track disease—ulcers, colitis

_____ Rheumatoid arthritis

_____ Migraine headaches

_____ Hyperthyroidism

_____ Lupus

_____ Trench mouth

_____ Bruxism (grinding of teeth)

_____ Canker and cold sores

_____ Gout

_____ Tuberculosis

_____ Thrombophlebitis

SELF-DIAGNOSIS

Physical Symptoms
(Check any that I frequently experience)

_____ Chest pain

_____ Chills

_____ Chronic illness

_____ Cold, sweaty palms

_____ Constipation or diarrhea

_____ Dry mouth

_____ Dry or itchy skin

_____ Fatigue

_____ Frequent illness, such as colds

_____ Frequent urination

_____ Headache

_____ Heavy perspiration

_____ Indigestion or heartburn

_____ Insomnia

_____ Jaw pain

_____ Nausea

_____ Rapid heartbeat

_____ Rapid, shallow breathing

_____ Ringing in ears

_____ Sexual dysfunction

_____ Stomachache

_____ Sweating excessively

_____ Swallowing problems

_____ Teeth grinding

_____ Tightness in your throat

_____ Trembling or shaking

_____ Weight change

Margaret's Toxic Stress

A physician friend of mine shares this story on the mind-body connection. "Margaret" was a European transplant to Florida, retired and living with her husband. The doctor was treating her for hypertension—high blood pressure. She started with a low dose of medication, but time after time, Margaret's blood pressure remained high. She told the doctor, it's my husband. He's hell to live with, always picking a fight with me, always angry. Three times, the doctor ratcheted up the dosage of Margaret's blood pressure medication.

Then one day Margaret came in, and her whole demeanor was different. She was smiling, she was relaxed, and her blood pressure was perfect. The doctor said, wow, what a difference, what's happened? Margaret said she had come home the day before and she had walked through the house and out to the front lawn where her husband was, and when she got there, he dropped dead. A day later, Margaret's stressor was gone and her blood pressure was normal.

Margaret's Toxic Stress

DIFFICULT LIFE SITUATION: Living with an abusive husband
PHYSICAL DAMAGE: High blood pressure
DEPRESSION: Mild
ANXIETY: Constant fear of her husband's anger
ACTION PLAN: Medication for high blood pressure until her stressor died

If my toxic stress patient "Claire" had filled in the blanks to identify her stressors, she would have written "medical problems." When we cleared those away, however, we identified another stressor in her life.

Claire's Toxic Stress

You know the old saying, "If you think a million dollars will solve all your problems, you never had a million dollars?" Claire had many millions at her disposal, yet stress made her physically ill and emotionally at wit's end.

Before her wealth, Claire had worked long hours at one or two jobs, whatever was required for this single parent to raise several children all on her own. As the children finished college, she knew she had succeeded, though those last years were hard. She teetered on burnout. At the height of her fatigue from so many stress-filled years of working and managing a family, she fell in love and married a man of huge wealth. Just when you would think she would be sighing with relief, she developed a series of medical problems. One after another. Her immune system was ravaged.

She had a gastrointestinal problem that caused her severe pain when she ate rich foods. Then she needed a hysterectomy, from which she did not heal easily. Unexplained severe pain in her groin was debilitating. She could not join her husband in the social format he most enjoyed—dining out at gourmet restaurants. And she could not pursue the activities that she enjoyed most—tennis and golf.

My experience with patients like Claire is that we have to clear up the medical issues before we can talk about the deep-seated matters such as why Claire was continuing to be so stressed when the old pressures were no longer there.

I became her agent, finding the doctors whose professional expertise Claire needed but also the doctors whose personalities and styles would best work for her. I begged doctor friends to spend a little extra time with her and explain fully the problems and the solutions. Fortunately, two doctors did that, and one just happened to have had a recent case similar to the unusual groin pain she had. Medication and rest solved it. The gastrointestinal problems also went away, with medication and the confidence the doctor communicated to her about its track record.

Finally, Claire could focus on the source of her ongoing stress. After living independently for so long, she struggled to cope with a new husband who imposed a variety of his own interests on her without understanding whether she shared them. He was buying a custom-made yacht and pressing her to make decisions on the interior design and furnishings. While some women might have been thrilled to have such an opportunity, the pressure to please her husband and his friends was more than Claire could handle. And the yacht meant more time away from home; she just wanted to stay put. She just could not bring herself to tell him about her unhappiness. So she lived with the stress of a multimillion-dollar lifestyle she did not like.

With help, she ultimately explained this to him, and, we can hope, they lived happily ever after, with a balance of tennis, gourmet dining, travel and yachting.

CLAIRE'S TOXIC STRESS

DIFFICULT LIFE SITUATION: Clinical burn-out from her previous profession; debilitating health problems, a demanding marriage after years of independence

PHYSICAL DAMAGE: Severe gastrointestinal problems (GERD), abdominal pain following surgery

DEPRESSION: Dysthymia, depressed over her health problems and her loss of ability to be physically active; sleep disorder

ANXIETY: Generalized anxiety disorder over her marriage, the yacht, compromises in her lifestyle; stress also related to her inability to play tennis and golf, which had been de-stressors in the past

ACTION PLAN: Psychotherapy; journaling; resolution of medical problems and monitoring of medications; negotiation with husband to diminish lifestyle stressors; identifying emotional distress and negative factors that affect her health; relaxation techniques; dedicating some time to herself to de-stress; exercise

MEDICATION: Paxil CR™ (antidepressant), Ambien® (sleep), Ativan® (antianxiety)

BIBLIOTHERAPY: *The Relaxation Response* (Benson), *Peace from Nervous Suffering* (Weekes), *Feeling Good: The New Mood Therapy* (Burns), *Getting the Love You Want* (Hendrix), *The Relaxation Stress Reduction Workbook* (Davis et al.)

Escaping into Negative Behaviors

Some people are innately equipped better to deal with stress. The rest of us have to learn how to cope. Sometimes we learn the hard way, and automatically react to stress with self-defeating behaviors. We get angry, for instance. In great frustration, with no easy answer in sight—husband and wife blame each other, the boss yells, road rage happens. When stress continues unabated, escape sounds good. So the stressed-out person attempts to escape from his bad feeling. Common escapes are alcohol and drugs ranging from marijuana and cocaine to prescription tranquilizers to over-the-counter sleeping aids. Add to that the anti-health behaviors of smoking, overeating and self-isolation. Not surprisingly, these behaviors compound the stress as they affect family, friends and coworkers.

SELF-DIAGNOSIS
Stress-Induced Feelings
Toxic stress is personal, but my mix of feelings may include these.
(Check all that apply)

____ Angry	____ Helpless	____ Panicky
____ Anxious	____ Hopeless	____ Resentful
____ Confused	____ Insecure	____ Sad
____ Defensive	____ Irritable	____ Suspicious
____ Depressed	____ Keyed up	____ Tired
____ Fearful	____ Lonely	____ Worried
____ Forgetful	____ Moody	____ Worthless
____ Frustrated		

SELF-DIAGNOSIS
Negative Behaviors
Identify my negative behaviors.
(Check all that apply)

____ Abuse of prescription medicine	
____ Anger—lashing out	____ Perfectionism
____ Excessive alcohol use	____ Physical abuse
____ Excessive crying	____ Procrastination
____ Illegal drug use	____ Self-isolation
____ Overeating/under-eating	____ Silence
	____ Smoking

Self-Diagnosis through Journaling

Carolyn's Toxic Stress

"Carolyn" was forty-six, an insurance executive in a high-stress work environment. Two events, happening within the same week, threw her into high stress. To save his job, her husband agreed to enter a detoxification program for drug addiction Carolyn had known nothing about. He was away and unavailable when the second event occurred, the September 11, 2001, terrorism. Carolyn's mother worked near the World Trade Center. Carolyn dialed and dialed, but could not find her mother for all of that first terrible day. Even though her mother turned out to be safe, Carolyn experienced flashbacks to her day of panic. When she came to see me, she had not slept in two weeks. I initially diagnosed Carolyn with acute stress disorder. As with many patients, however, I could see that she was not a one-issue case.

CAROLYN'S TOXIC STRESS

DIFFICULT LIFE SITUATION: Panic over mother's safety on Sept. 11; husband's drug addiction; childhood sexual abuse that came to light during therapy

PHYSICAL DAMAGE: Frequent colds, a dermatologic disorder, migraine headaches

DEPRESSION: Dysthymia, sadness, sleeplessness, fatigue

ANXIETY: Acute stress disorder, panic disorder, chronic worry; flashbacks to Sept. 11, flashbacks to childhood sexual abuse

ACTION PLAN: Psychotherapy, journaling, cognitive restructuring, relaxation techniques to handle panic disorder; exploration of childhood sexual trauma and resolution of anger related to family denial of abuse; changing negative self-talk, developing better self-esteem

MEDICATION: Zoloft® (antidepressant), Ativan® (antianxiety), Ambien® (sleep)

BIBLIOTHERAPY: *The Feeling Good Handbook* (Burns), *Ten Days to Self-Esteem!* (Burns)

As I learned more about Carolyn, I understood that anxiety was a way of life for her. Yes, the flashbacks to September 11 had debilitated her, but, truly, she had lived with anxiety most of her life. She was, by nature, a worrier. She told me that in previous therapy she had found keeping a journal gave her comfort, so journaling became a centerpiece to our work together. She was articulate and self-insightful. I found her journal to be haunting.

Journaling is an excellent way for you to self-diagnose your stress, and over time to identify patterns of stressors and your responses that may not be so apparent at the beginning of your journey into change.

Entire books have been written about journaling, but I take a simple, undemanding approach to it. Every day, or every other day, you simply write down your thoughts, feelings, emotions, etc. You do need to establish a time and place for journaling, and commit to it. You also will want to find a comfortable, quiet spot in which you can think and write freely without distraction.

I recommend stream-of-conscious writing. Don't worry about complete sentences or punctuation or rules of grammar. Just let your thoughts flow onto paper. In your journal, write your impressions of the day, how you feel, emotions, issues, events, pressures—whatever comes to mind when you review your day. At the end of the week, review your work and look for those patterns of stressors and your effectiveness in dealing with them. What were your "triggers"? How did you cope?

Journaling is a well-researched and proven technique. Psychologists refer to it as "self-monitoring." Research shows that journaling is cathartic—it makes you feel better—as well self-diagnostic. Seeing how many negative thoughts you had in a given week can be instructive. An article I read recently cited research on a group of journalers. Of all their comments, eighty-six percent of what they wrote was negative. When you realize how much time you invest in negative thought, you are motivated to seek a more positive outlook You should be committed to changing those automatic negative self-statements. Think about how you can change them into more positive ones. (More on this in Step 4: Think with the Bright Side of Your Brain.)

Carolyn's Journal

Reviewing some of Carolyn's journal during therapy gave me much insight into Carolyn's problems. Carolyn's thoughts emerged in verse or couplets. Such poetry is not necessary; it is just how Carolyn did it. She gave me permission to share some examples of it with you:

> My tunnel is empty
> Quiet and cold
>
> Constructed by others
> But the crevices I did mold
>
> Wide-eyed, shivering and scared
> I possess a child's stance
>
> Frightened of the beginning
> So far away is the ending
>
> Stuck somewhere in between
> With nothing ever mending
>
> Days and nights are long
> My body has grown weary
>
> I feel the need to move someplace
> I just can't see very clearly
>
> If I should find the light switch
> Would I really want to use it?
>
> What would I find next to me?
> In this never-ending snake pit
>
> Maybe I'll stay here
> Just awhile longer
>
> To have a light in my tunnel
> My soul must be much stronger

Journaling Provides Insights

The next excerpt from a bright, articulate man in his thirties was written during therapy in which he hoped to gain insight into his family history, professional lethargy, and problems of trust and commitment in his personal life. He believed journaling to be a great technique for him, and gave me permission to share this with you.

"I am the younger of two children of what may have appeared on the surface to be an average middle-class family. My father was a high school teacher, and my mother worked in sales at a department store. Our family unraveled when I was about six, and here I sit at almost thirty-three, recounting a lifetime of painful events and hoping that I'll finally learn how to leave them behind.

"Don't get me wrong—there have been, and are now, many positive things in my life. Nonetheless, I've lived a life thus far where loneliness, despair and pain seem to be nearby companions. Just as nearby have been deep-seated feelings of optimism and faith. The net result of this mix, from my own viewpoint, is a life full of tremendous promise yet to be realized—a life of treading water, waiting and wanting to flourish, but not knowing how to free itself from what feels like self-imposed bondage."

Over marathon weekends of writing he gained great insight into his past, his own personality dynamics and his sexual identity.

HOW TO JOURNAL

1. Select a comfortable location where you can write without distractions or interruptions. Turn the phone and TV off.
2. Write in longhand, or on the computer.
3. Keep your journal in a private place. It's for you alone.
4. Try to write daily, even if only briefly; if not, write every other day.
5. Write in the stream-of-conscious mode, flowing your thoughts onto paper without concern for complete sentences or punctuation. Or whatever feels comfortable to you.
6. Start with whatever pops in your mind first as you mentally review your day.
7. If you're stuck for something to write, try these cues:
    Stress today: low/high, why?
    Stress today: how you coped
    Emotions: love/anger, safety/fear, happiness/sadness
    Attitudes: confidence/insecurity, assertive/passive, confident/unsure, strong/weak
    Behaviors: strong/weak, quick/slow, effective/ineffective, productive/unproductive

Relationships (friends, family): healthy/unhealthy, progressing/ regressing, threatened/secure

Workplace: workload/overload, reasonable time/overtime, fitting in/ not fitting in

Health: good/bad, stress-related/stress overcome

Wishes and hopes: for today and for the future

8. Review your work at week's end. Look for patterns of stressors and behavior, especially for insight into how you are creating your own stress.

9. Write a short summary of what you conclude from your review.

Summary

Stress threatens our physical and mental health more seriously and complexly than most people comprehend. The mind-body connection is now documented by great bodies of research. A first step at overcoming toxic stress is analyzing and identifying the stressors in your life, your physical and emotional symptoms, your feelings under stress and your negative behaviors fueled by stress. Journaling provides personal insights into your life, personality and problems that may not be immediately obvious. It is also a therapeutic release of some feelings, and a vehicle to guide you through a maze of thoughts and feelings that can lead you to self-discovery.

In this step you self-diagnosed:

Toxic Stress	Your Difficult Life Situation
Stress-Related Diseases and Conditions	Physical Symptoms
Stress-Induced Feelings	Negative Behaviors

Strategies and Techniques

Journaling is the strategy that you may wish to record as a first entry in your Action Plan to Recovery. Strategies and techniques follow each chapter summary and are repeated in a complete Action Plan format following Step 7.

❑ Journaling   Place _____   How often? _____

❑ Bibliotherapy _____

Step 2

Dig Out of Depression

Enjoy life's 'puddles'. Make cheerfulness, outrageousness and playfulness new priorities for your life. You can feel good for no reason at all.
—Anthony Robbins

Step 2

Dig Out of Depression

Gina's Toxic Stress

The wife of a high-level executive came to me, feeling the stress of a move from the North to Florida, away from family and friends. As her husband dove into an exciting new job, she was trapped at home with young children. She was bored and lonely. She gained weight, which made her even unhappier. She snapped at her husband, who returned the favor, the couple arguing most bitterly over whether to have more children. "Gina" hated her new life and felt unsupported and un-loved.

Beginning with Gina, I will show you how depression festers in the toxic stress matrix and how you can dig out of depression using research-proven techniques of cognitive psychology, behavior modification, relaxation, creative problem-solving and, in some cases, prescription or herbal medication.

GINA'S TOXIC STRESS

DIFFICULT LIFE SITUATION: Isolation from old friends and family, conflicts with her husband over more children, and financial problems

PHYSICAL DAMAGE: Fibromyalgia, female reproductive disorder, back pain

DEPRESSION: Dysthymia
ANXIETY: Generalized anxiety disorder
ACTION PLAN: Psychotherapy; marital therapy; cognitive restructuring; an exercise and diet plan; journaling; problem-solving to bring more intimacy to her marriage; referral to medical sources for diagnosis of an autistic child; career counseling to assist financially and give her new social contacts and a social support system
MEDICATION: Zoloft® (antidepressant)
BIBLIOTHERAPY: *Feeling Good* (Burns), *The New Sugar Busters* (Steward)

Stress can lead to depression, or a depressed person can stumble into a stressful time, or the persistent dysfunction of depression can create stress when it interferes with daily social or professional functioning. Whichever way, depression is a core element of toxic stress.

Everyone feels depressed at times, when a loved one dies, for example. But depression goes beyond that short-term, normal grieving response. Depression is a change in your brain chemistry that affects your thinking, emotions, sleep, self-esteem, productivity, appetite, sex life and day-to-day functioning. About 20 million adults in America suffer from depression each year. Approximately one-fourth of all women and twelve percent of all men will experience an episode of major depression some time in their lives. That works out to about one in six American adults having depression sometime in their lives. It is why depression is sometimes called the common cold of mental illness.

There are many degrees of depression including clinical or major depression, dysthymia, cyclothymia and bipolar disorder. Cyclothymia is a milder form of bipolar disorder. Although this book does not address the more complex bipolar disorder, there are a number of useful books on the topic.

Stress-linked clinical depression and dysthymia are frequently about loss, and the inability to cope with everyday or special-event stressors that come along at the same time. Sometimes the loss is obvious—your husband dies and your stress persists beyond the expected stages of grief. Or, you are laid off from your dream job, or you become disabled and can no longer drive or walk unaided. Other times, the loss is less apparent. Your only child goes off to college. You find yourself in deep financial trouble. Or, as Gina, you lose your support system.

She felt stress trapped with the children at home, but underlying it was the loss of her familiar and comfortable life in the North, people and activities that provided balance and stress relief.

One highly regarded view of depression, the "cognitive triad," comes from Dr. Aaron T. Beck. Dr. Beck revolutionized psychotherapy. He has been listed as one of the ten most influential individuals in the history of American psychiatry and one of the five most influential psychotherapists of all time. When he joined the Department of Psychiatry of the University of Pennsylvania in 1954, he initially conducted research into the psychoanalytic theories of depression, but he found the approaches flawed. This led to his development of a new theoretical-clinical approach, which he called cognitive therapy, and later the cognitive-behavioral matrix. Though originally focusing solely on patients with depression, cognitive-behavioral therapy now is used in treatment of many kinds of mental disorders.

Dr. Beck theorized that depression-prone people have negative views of themselves, their environments and their futures. Their negative thinking skews their perspective and leads to a negative sense of self, and depression.

Still another theory, the "hopelessness theory" of depression, built on the helplessness theory, argues that some people have a thinking style that causes them to assume the worst when confronted with a negative event. The "helplessness theory" of depression came from Dr. Martin Seligman. In this theory, uncontrollable events lead to the belief that behavior cannot change outcomes. Motivation, problem-solving ability and emotions are negatively affected. This cognitive vulnerability increases the risk for depression, according to this research.

Other major research on depression came from Dr. Albert Ellis who said irrational thoughts and belief systems create irrational behaviors

Most theories on depression lead to treatment options that include cognitive and behavioral changes—changing the way people think about themselves and their circumstances and how they behave. You can use the principles of cognitive behavioral psychology to diminish depression that is part of your toxic stress.

The symptoms and causes of depression differ from person to person, but those in the accompanying boxes are among the most common.

SELF-DIAGNOSIS

Symptoms of Depression

If you demonstrate at least five of these conditions, if they have persisted for at least two weeks and interfere with your daily functioning at home or at work, you may be clinically depressed. Call your doctor and make an appointment right away if you are thinking about suicide. Check those that apply.

_____ Persistent sadness

_____ Sleeping too much or too little

_____ Poor appetite and weight loss, or increased appetite and weight gain

_____ Loss of pleasure and interest in usual activities, including sex

_____ Irritability, restlessness, agitation

_____ Physical hyperactivity

_____ Difficulty concentrating, remembering or making decisions

_____ Fatigue or loss of energy

_____ Feelings of worthlessness, hopelessness or inappropriate guilt

_____ Thoughts of death or suicide

_____ Diminished ability to think or concentrate

The Beck Depression Inventory is a proven diagnostic tool. You can take this test at regular intervals to assess depression levels. The Zung Depression Inventory is a similar tool, and some adaptations of it have just twenty questions and easy-to-understand scoring. (Ask your doctor or psychologist for the tests; they are also easy to find through a search on the Web.) The National Mental Health Association sponsors an on-line depression screening test that is just nine questions long. It is a quick barometer to measure the severity of the down feelings you might be experiencing (www.depression-screening.org).

These symptoms show up in conditions other than depression, as well. People with thyroid disorders, for example, might have the same fatigue, irritability, weight changes, blue feelings. It is a good idea to get a thorough medical check-up when you identify these symptoms.

Factors of Depression

What contributes to depression? It is not entirely understood, though there are clusters of factors, some of which parallel the toxic stress matrix.

Difficult Life Situation: Stressful events such as the death of a loved one, divorce, marital cheating, financial strains, relocating or other significant loss—these are common stress-linked sources of depression and a core element of toxic stress.

Anxiety and Negative Thinking Patterns: People who are anxious, pessimistic, have low self-esteem or feel they have little control over life events are more likely to develop depression. Anxiety is a core element of toxic stress.

Physical Damage and Certain Diseases: Diseases or conditions such as cancer, heart disease, Parkinson's disease, Alzheimer's disease, diabetes and hormonal disorders can trigger clinical depression. Physical damage is a core element of toxic stress.

Excessive Alcohol Consumption, Drug Abuse: Alcohol dependence can lead to depression, and depression can lead to self-medication with alcohol and drugs.

Highly Competitive Environments: Where the pressure to achieve is relentless or unforgiving, as in college when a student is graded on performance at every turn, depression is more likely to occur.

Abuse or Crime Victim: This goes back to the research that shows that people subjected to early childhood trauma have changed brain chemistry that makes them more vulnerable to stress and depression. Other research shows the changed brain chemistry of crime victims, including of domestic abuse.

Imbalance of Brain Chemicals Called Neurotransmitters: Depressed people lack sufficient serotonin and possibly the neurotransmitters dopamine and norepinephrine. Medication, diet/exercise and therapy can restore those levels.

Family History of Depression: A genetic history of clinical depression increases your risk of developing depression.

Certain Medications: Some medication can contribute to depression. Incorrect dosages of Xanax®, Valium®, Klonopin® and Ativan® are identified as contributing to depression.

Birth of a Child and Other Hormonal Changes: Ten to twenty percent of women develop postpartum depression, up to a year following childbirth.

Gender: Women are more likely to become depressed than men.

Sadly, we are diagnosing more and more children with depression. Previously, we did not consider a prepubescent child as having sufficient complexities of life and intellect to experience depression. Now we are diagnosing depression in children as young as five.

The good news is that depression is highly treatable. More than eight out of ten people with depression can be helped. Even better, for people who were relatively happy and healthy before a life-changing, stressful event occurred, the prognosis for turning around the depression is very good. Scientific studies show that brief short-term therapy, lasting eight to twenty weeks, is often effective.

Jim's Toxic Stress

Many depressions stem from the loss of a personal relationship, as in the death of a spouse or child, or divorce, or the break-up of a romance. On a slightly different level, I worked with one patient who was angry and depressed about the loss of his sex life. "Jim" had been in a serious relationship with a woman for about two years. Then he discovered he had a sexually transmitted disease, and, worse, she had knowingly exposed him to it. The relationship ended, precipitating a depressive episode.

But what he was most angry and depressed over was that his future was so changed by his new medical condition. Before falling in love with his ex-girlfriend he had led a flirtatious life as a handsome, sexy tennis pro. He had prided himself on his attractiveness and his prowess in bed. Now that part of his life was gone, and he was experiencing psychologically induced impotency.

At the tennis club, Jim could not do his job as well as usual because he could not clear the anger and depression from his head. He exhibited all the elements of toxic stress.

JIM'S TOXIC STRESS

DIFFICULT LIFE SITUATION: Loss of a long-term relationship
PHYSICAL DAMAGE: Sexually transmitted disease, muscle injury, sexual dysfunction
DEPRESSION: Symptoms of a major depressive episode—experiencing withdrawal, sadness, apathy, lethargy and loss of joy
ANXIETY: Relationship conflicts, and a muscle injury that jeopardized his present job and worry about his future career
ACTION PLAN: Psychotherapy; anger management; rebuilding of self-esteem; medical treatment for muscle injury and the STD; daily church attendance and meditation; problem-solving that included exploring legal options against the ex-girlfriend
MEDICATION: Zoloft® (antidepressant), Xanax® (antianxiety)

Daily Mass had been Jim's source of solace in the past. He found comfort in prayer and ritual, which provided a measure of relaxation and relief from the stress hormones. Outside of the sanctuary, however, his anger made him want revenge, to exact some financial penalty from his girlfriend for betraying him and knowingly exposing him to disease. After investigating his options and talking with an attorney, he concluded his chances of winning were very low, and he gave up on that idea. The process of analyzing it and ruling it out, however, turned out to be quite therapeutic. He moved on with his life.

Social Stigma of Depression

Many patients with toxic stress want to deny the depression component because of the stigma still connected to the label. Fortunately, the public's understanding of depression is improving. In recent years, celebrities such as *60 Minutes* co-editor Mike Wallace, humorist Art Buchwald and Pulitzer Prize–winning author William Styron *(Sophie's Choice, Darkness Visible: A Memoir of Madness)* have talked in public about their struggles with depression. On a TV documentary about his bouts with severe clinical depression, Wallace said, "The sunshine means nothing to you at all. The seasons, friends, good food mean nothing. All you focus on is yourself and how bad you feel." The image is of a much different

Mike Wallace from the self-confident and assertive TV personality, but the important underlying message is that with treatment he overcame depression and now in his early eighties is still on network television.

In the much-acclaimed HBO television series *The Sopranos,* Tony Soprano receives therapy and medication for depression and panic attacks, again heightening public perception of mental illness (though you certainly don't have to be a mobster like Tony Soprano to be depressed). In TV's days of yore, Lucy and Desi's friend Fred Murtz had depression, as did Ed Asner's character Lou Grant and Sue Ellen Ewing of *Dallas.*

When Depression Creates Self-Danger

Depression is a serious condition, and it can spiral down to danger. If you have suicidal thoughts, you must get professional treatment right away. This is how it happened to my patient "Larry."

Larry's Toxic Stress

Larry's wife persuaded him to see me, because he had threatened suicide. Larry had been very successful in business in the Northwest, had sold his companies and retired at an early age to Florida. He and his wife expected to live not just comfortably here but luxuriously.

But Larry had always been a risk-taker, and he had invested heavily in high-tech stocks and others that plummeted in value in recent years. In effect, he lost it all.

LARRY'S TOXIC STRESS

DIFFICULT LIFE SITUATION: Losing his fortune in the stock market, history of child abuse by an angry father

PHYSICAL DAMAGE: Chronic pain from an accident and previous work injuries, migraine headaches, significant weight loss

DEPRESSION: Major depressive episode

ANXIETY: Chronic anxiety and worry about his finances, selling his home, providing for his family and maintaining his marriage

ACTION PLAN: Psychotherapy; referral to a neurologist for chronic pain management and antidepressant medication for his depressive symptoms; daily walks with his dogs for exercise; marital therapy; rebuilding his self-esteem and creating more intimacy with his wife; and problem-solving that included turning over the stressful money matters to his wife, vocational counseling and creating a plan for a new business venture

MEDICATION: Effexor® (antidepressant)

BIBLIOTHERAPY: *Feeling Good: The New Mood Therapy* (Burns), *Intimate Connections* (Burns)

Larry's wife convinced him to seek treatment. Any time someone threatens suicide, you must get them to a professional to assess their condition.

For Larry, and for most people who are severely depressed, there is little chance of effective problem-solving until the debilitating symptoms of depression are relieved. We had to make Larry feel better and think straighter and have more energy before he could create a new business and start over.

Correcting Distorted Thinking

In psychotherapy I help patients first to recognize and understand why they are depressed. And then I help them realize how they perpetuate the depression through their own distorted thinking patterns. Cognitive behavioral treatment of depression applies specific, scientifically proven strategies focused first on changing negative thinking patterns, then on changing behavior and, for patients feeling stress or anxiety as well, the use of imagery, meditation and relaxation procedures to calm themselves and get control of those stress hormones threatening their physical health.

Depression festers because of how you think of your situation without a healthy perspective. I tell my patients, be aware, and beware, of distorted thinking. With depression, people slip into negative mental ruts characterized mostly by hopelessness, or a sense of worthlessness. To dig out of this depression, you have to realize you are being unfair and untruthful to yourself. Depressed people can be very creative in how they do this. Here is my list of various categories of distorted thinking, adapted from the work of Dr. Aaron Beck, David Burns, Albert Ellis, other therapists and my own practice.

Kinds of Distorted Thinking

FILTERING Focusing on the negative details while filtering out the positive.

OVERGENERALIZATION The "always" and "never" realms. Making broad conclusions based on narrow evidence. Usually with negative, hopelessness or helplessness aspects.

MIND READING Jumping to a conclusion about someone's thoughts or plans.

CATASTROPHIZING Exaggerating errors or problems, both past and future. "What if" statements set up the gloomy, tragic or debilitating view.

ALL OR NOTHING THINKING Black or white, never a gray or middle ground.

PERSONALIZATION Thinking that everything that people do or say is a reaction to you. Obsessive self-comparison.

EMOTIONAL REASONING Believing that your negative feelings are correct. If you feel stupid today, you must be stupid.

FALLACY OF FAIRNESS You incorrectly assume you are the superior judge of what is fair, but life is full of different interpretations of what is fair.

SHOULD STATEMENTS You have rigid rules by which you and others should behave. You are unforgiving when you or they stray.

BLAMING Holding other people responsible for your feelings, or taking responsibility for the feelings of other people.

GLOBAL LABELING Attaching an over-generalized label to yourself or others—stereotyping.

SELF-RIGHTEOUSNESS You strive constantly to prove that your opinions and actions are correct.

MARTYRDOM You expect your sacrifice and self-denial to pay off, and you are bitter when the reward doesn't come.

FALLACY OF CHANGE Just because you wish someone to change, and do your part to make it happen, change is not guaranteed.

To help my patients overcome negative automatic thoughts, I recommend the Triple-Column Technique developed by Dr. David Burns and widely used by psychologists and other therapists. This is a proven technique of cognitive restructuring, or reframing.

In the Triple-Column Technique you write down your negative automatic thoughts in the first column. In the second column you challenge what you have written—as a devil's advocate might point out the distortions you have made. In the third column, you rewrite your thoughts from your new perspective. Here is an example from the workplace.

THE TRIPLE-COLUMN TECHNIQUE		
NEGATIVE THOUGHT	DEVIL'S ADVOCATE	NEW TRUTH
Automatic and exaggerated	**Identifying the distortion**	**Kinder to yourself**
"I procrastinated again, and now everyone's paying for it, because we missed the project deadline. I'm always screwing up."	"This was a team project, and we are all accountable for the outcome. My mistakes were just part of the reason we missed deadline. Making mistakes does not mean I always make mistakes and am, therefore, a screw-up."	"I made some mistakes, but I can learn from them, including how to work better as a team."

For situations of ongoing depression or other difficult times, such as during a divorce, keep your Triple-Column List handy. And when you hear yourself thinking one of those distorted thoughts, pick up the list and reread it. Listen for the absolutes, which are rarely absolute—the "never," "always," "totally" phrases. Listen for the labels and the other kinds of distorted thinking.

The Brain Chemistry of Depression

As a cognitive-behavioral therapist, I help patients to correct distorted cognitions or irrational thoughts. Research shows us that therapy can actually change the chemistry of the brain, which is required in the treatment of depression because depression is believed to be related to a deficiency of one or more of the neu-rotransmitters serotonin, norepinephrine and dopamine.

Serotonin produces feelings of well-being, peacefulness, confidence. A deficiency of serotonin produces anxiety, irritability, insomnia and a craving for carbohydrates. Norepinephrine is a neurotransmitter that increases energy and alertness. Dopamine is a neurotransmitter associated with the feeling of well-be-ing, and possibly short-term memory.

If you are mildly depressed or experiencing only occasional "down" days, cognitive restructuring strategies such as the Triple-Column Technique may be enough. A support group can be helpful, too. For moderate or more serious depression, however, you need to understand the chemical imbalance behind depression and why I believe medication is often critical to recovery.

Serotonin is a star of depression research, and the basis of most antide-pressant medication. In a chain-link process from its billions of neurons, the brain sends serotonin through the nervous system to sites that we know play roles in the symptoms of depression. Serotonin affects mood, appetite, emotion and sleep—all areas negatively affected in persons with depression.

In depressed patients serotonin and other neurotransmitters get sent out and pass from neuron (nerve cell) to neuron. But something goes wrong, and they are sent back, where the body destroys them. The net result is not enough serotonin. Research strongly regards a lack of serotonin to be the most common chemical imbalance behind depression.

Medications

The two most commonly prescribed types of antidepressants are selective seroto-nin re-uptake inhibitors (SSRIs), such as Prozac®, Zoloft®, Paxil CR™ (con-trolled release), Celexa™, and Lexapro™, and tricyclic antidepressants (TCAs), such as Elavil® and Tofranil®. Controlled release medications call for a single dosage per day, reducing the possibility of missing a dose. The term *re-uptake inhibitors* means that these medications make more serotonin available to the brain. Other atypical antidepressants include Remeron®, Serzone® and Luvox®. Ask your physician about the one that is appropriate for you.

Selective serotonin and norepinephrine re-uptake inhibitors (SSNRIs) are another medication option, generally with fewer side effects than the TCAs, and, finally, bupropion, sold under the name Wellbutrin®, is an antidepressant classified as a dopamine re-uptake blocking compound. Wellbutrin® recently was approved in controlled-release form. It works on the neurotransmitters dopamine and norepinephrine and is highly regarded because it is less likely to produce sexual dysfunction than some other drugs. Effexor® works on the re-uptake of norepinephrine, serotonin and, to a lesser extent, dopamine.

Psychiatrists often prescribe combinations of medications to address multiple factors, for instance, co-existing anxiety and depression, as we have it in toxic stress.

Medication Therapy

Some psychologists and mental health workers encourage their clients to work on their issues without the use of antianxiety or antidepressant drugs. Generally speaking, I advocate the use of appropriate psychotropic medication for persons with anxiety or depression. The medications serve as a "jump-start" for therapy, getting the patient to the point where he or she can think more clearly and engage in the talk therapy and learn the relaxation skills and other techniques that are critical to recovery. When they begin to feel better, they can focus more on therapy and less on the discomfort of physical symptoms.

In most states, psychologists are not authorized to prescribe medicines, and therefore I work closely with psychiatrists, primary care doctors and specialists who do have this knowledge and authorization. We become partners in the patient's care.

Many patients resist my suggestion for medications. They say, "Oh, no, I'm not that bad!" Or, "Oh, no, not a psychiatrist!" I often have an educational element to my sessions, explaining the newest medications and how new medicines have fewer side effects and are not addicting, and assuaging fears about psychiatrists.

Meta-analysis—the analysis of multiple research findings, taken as a whole—has proven that the combination of psychotropic medication and psychotherapy is significantly more effective than medication alone or therapy alone. That is the best argument—medication plus therapy works best.

Some recent research indicates that some doctors may not be prescribing antidepressant and antianxiety medication in dosages high enough to produce ideal results. If you do not feel better, ask about the dosage and consider a referral to a psychiatrist.

The latest research focuses on the role of cortisol in patients with depression. Studies have found that as many as half of people with depression also have elevated levels of the stress hormone cortisol. In fact, research is under way at the University of San Francisco to determine if stress and elevated cortisol levels actually cause depression in some people.

As evidence of a further link between cortisol and depression, animal research shows that long-term exposure to cortisol (stress) damages certain serotonin-producing nerves. The ensuing logic is that too much cortisol reduces serotonin and makes you depressed.

Once most people understand how basic the chemical imbalance of depression is, they are more receptive to trying medication, most effectively in conjunction with psychotherapy. Research shows that antidepressants speed recovery in both severe and moderate depression. These drugs are not addictive and have fewer side effects than earlier antidepressants. So if you are sufficiently concerned about your down feelings, talk to your doctor about medication. And be prepared to stick with it for awhile—you may feel better in just a month, but you may need medication for nine months to a year in order to prevent relapse.

The Herbals and Other Over-the-Counter Choices

If, for whatever reason, you want to try nonprescription alternatives, you also have some choices. Research is mixed, and none of these has Federal Drug Administration approval as drugs. They are considered food supplements. Under no condition should you take both prescription antidepressants and herbals. You would risk significant side effects.

Doctors in Europe have prescribed SAM-e for depression and other conditions for more than twenty years. In the United States it is classified as a nutritional supplement and is available over-the-counter. SAM-e is a natural substance produced in the human body from amino acids and has some kind of role in the function of neurotransmitters, including serotonin and dopamine. Similar to prescription antidepressants SAM-e has an effectiveness time lag of four to five weeks but none of the side effects such as sexual dysfunction or insomnia.

Saint-John's-wort is sold over-the-counter, too, but do not expect immediate results with this one, either. Saint-John's-wort is a bushy, low-growing plant with yellow flowers. In medicinal form, effectiveness kicks in at six to eight weeks. This substance appears to prevent the destruction of serotonin and to increase the availability of dopamine and norepinephrine. Some research shows it to be no more effective than a placebo, but some people swear by it. Be sure to ask about interactions with other drugs you may be taking, because of potential liver damage, and follow dosages carefully.

If you experience five or more depression symptoms every day for two weeks or more, you need to see a physician and discuss medication and therapy. If you identify with some of the symptoms periodically, or are mildly depressed, you will find more good ideas for coping in this book. But be vigilant, because people bombarded by stressors of contemporary life can slip into more serious depression. That's why we have an entire step called Dig Out of Depression.

How to Start Feeling Better

After analyzing what caused your depression or gloomy outlook, the next step is action. Action is hard when you are depressed. We have already established that you may be lethargic, tired and have a hard time making decisions. Yet that is when you push yourself. The first line of treatment is to keep moving. To dig out of depression's downward spiral, you must dig into something more positive.

I recommend the Pleasure File, as shown in this next profile of toxic stress.

Olivia's Toxic Stress

My patient "Olivia" suffers from recurring depression. A stressful event or situation will occur and she will relapse into depression. She deals with it by going to bed. Changes in sleep patterns are a common symptom of depression. Olivia goes to bed and does not come out of her bedroom for days. She crawls deeper and deeper into her own shell. She is one of those extra-vulnerable people who suffered child abuse and, in Olivia's case, also an abusive earlier marriage.

Her current husband encourages her to get up out of bed, to not let herself slip farther. Together, Olivia and I created her Pleasure File. I asked, What gives you the most pleasure? When do you feel best about yourself?

She likes to go to the library. We put that on a 3 by 5 index card. She likes to take walks. Another card. A weekend getaway—that would help repair the relationship with the husband, too. She also likes having friends over for lunch or dinner. Her husband does the cooking, so she is left with the less-stressful "duty" of conversation. That was a wonderful addition to her Pleasure File.

The Pleasure File works for people with depression because it takes the stress or pressure out of deciding what to do. The answers are already there on the index cards—or posted as 10 Pleasures on your refrigerator door. It's just a matter of selecting one. Many times, when you change your behavior—even when you are forcing yourself—your mood improves.

When you are feeling very down, you turn to the index box or posted pleasures and choose. To each their own, of course—but you will find some suggestions for Pleasure File entries on the next page.

OLIVIA'S TOXIC STRESS

DIFFICULT LIFE SITUATION: Minor stressors affecting her disproportionately; previous domestic abuse, violence and childhood abuse

PHYSICAL DAMAGE: Frequent migraine headaches, arthritis

DEPRESSION: A history of depressive episodes with psychotic features and hospitalizations for clinical depression

ANXIETY: Generalized anxiety disorder

ACTION PLAN: Psychotherapy; referral to a psychiatrist for appropriate medications; journaling; exercise and beach walking; cognitive restructuring; assertiveness training; marital therapy, and problem-solving that led to a volunteer job to combat her tendency to withdraw

MEDICATION: Abilify™ (atypical antipsychotic), Wellbutrin® (antidepressant), Klonopin® (antianxiety)

BIBLIOTHERAPY: *Feeling Good: The New Mood Therapy* (Burns), *Ten Steps to Self-Esteem* (Burns), *When I Say No, I Feel Guilty* (Smith)

PLEASURE FILE POSSIBILITIES

Go to lunch with friends

Hike a trail

Walk the neighborhood

Go to a concert

Get a facial or manicure

Call a friend or relative

Go camping

Get a massage

Work out at the gym

Take a weekend trip
    with a friend

Go to the zoo

Read

Drop in on pick-up basket-
    ball or volleyball game

Try aromatherapy

Walk your dog

Turn to your hobbies—
    sewing, photography, art,
    crafts, gardening,
    scrapbooking

Shop to treat yourself

Volunteer to help others

The Pleasure File is an easy-to-understand example of behavior modification. Treatment of depression often includes these three thrusts: (1)changing thinking, (2) behavior modification, (3) calming/relaxation. Olivia changed her behavior by getting out of bed and having friends over for lunch. Putting that foot on the floor, nevertheless, was very hard for Olivia. She felt she did not deserve to feel pleasure, and she had no energy.

Keep Moving

Activity is extremely important in confronting depression. You have to stop that downward change spiral. You have to get the brain back to its business of producing serotonin and into the habit of accepting pleasure. It helps to have a friend or partner who understands how important activity is to the mitigation of depression. Olivia's husband knew to encourage her to get out of bed. The Pleasure File gave him a mechanism to turn to whenever depression returned and he saw that "first sign" of Olivia of taking to her bed. If you are vulnerable to depression, tell a friend there will be a time when you will need a push out the door into a more active environment.

Ultimately, Olivia found personal reward in a volunteer job—at the local hospital. The job gave her a purpose and a little time off from her marriage.

Art, Music and Dance Therapy

For Olivia, it was a volunteer job that removed her from her sources of stress. For many people, the answer lies in the arts. Art, music and dance are creative endeavors, and engaging in them coaxes the brain into different modes. There is order, or lack of order, for your brain to consider. You call on yourself to be imaginative. All this stimulates some self-healing.

Art therapy may be simply your self-expression in paint, clay, collage, metal, wood or mixed media. You may find art therapy classes in your community; these are usually directed by people with both art and mental health credentials. In those classes, you would use the art to express your feelings or circumstances and to reflect on them. Colors and shapes take on new significance.

Music can relax us so deeply that hospitals have used it for more than seventy-five years to ease patients' anxiety, relieve tension and brighten mood. It is another therapy that is widely accessible and adaptable to most any taste in music. Some research shows that music pleasant to an individual's ear can stimulate endorphins and therefore bring calm, content and feelings of general well-being—all excellent relief from toxic stress that is laced with depression. Another study shows that you can reduce your stress-induced cortisol level by as much as twenty-five percent when you listen to music for more than fifteen minutes daily. How easy is that?

Some people find CDs of nature's sounds to be soothing. There is a wide variety on the market, from ocean waves coming ashore to birds in the rain forest. Particularly if you are an outdoors person, a natural sounds CD might be an excellent mental retreat for you.

Dance is still another artistic outlet, affording opportunity for expression as well as exercise. It is difficult to feel depressed when you are dancing. Take a class, buy a dance workout video, or just boogie in the den.

Light Therapy

Just as you might not have thought of the arts as therapeutic for people living with depression, you may be surprised by this latest entry in the treatment options.

Research now supports the theory that a loss of light sometimes correlates with depression and that increasing your exposure to light can diminish depression. Much of the research was on people with Seasonal Affective Disorder (SAD) who became depressed in winter when daylight hours are shortened, or they were otherwise deprived of access to light. Night shift people often have this problem.

Enter the light box as treatment. Light boxes come in many shapes, sizes, power ranges and price ranges, though the best are over $150. Not just any light will do. Therapeutic light must be at least 10,000 lux. Lux is an international standard measurement for illumination. With a 10,000 lux, full-spectrum light box that sits on your desktop, you would strive for twenty to thirty minutes each morning, about the time you might read the newspaper. Some users also add twenty to thirty minutes in early evening to extend their wakefulness.

If cost is not an issue for you, the light box is an option to try. Even newer—and odder—is some evidence that the same light cast on the back of the knees rather than the face and upper body will produce the same positive effects.

Pet Therapy

I once saw a cartoon that said, "Lord, make me the person my dog thinks I am." My coauthor Patty is a "dog person." Her two Miniature Schnauzers reward her with unconditional love and attention. It is hard to stay angry or unhappy or stressed-out when she comes home to two tail-wagging dogs who are ecstatic at her arrival and eager to get their treats and sit in her lap. Walking a dog is an excellent activity for a person with depression—you get companionship and exercise at the same time. Dogs are pretty good listeners, too. Whatever you say, you're always right!

Relaxation

Another treatment for depression—relaxation—is especially important for people with toxic stress because they are coping with both depression and anxiety in varying degrees. You can diminish the effects of both depression and anxiety through relaxation techniques that give the brain and body a time-out from all that troubles you. In the next chapter you will find some excellent relaxation exercises, meditation, yoga, CDs or tapes and other suggestions to help you relax and tune out your demons, worries and doubts.

Sleep, Diet and Exercise

Sleep is more critical to our health than most of us realize. We need seven to eight hours of deep sleep a night in order for our bodies to restore cells. Some depressed people sleep too much, some sleep too little. If you are sleeping too little, pay special attention to the tips for sound sleep in Step 6: Commit to Health and Wellness. That chapter also explains the benefits of diet and exercise that stimulate brain activity.

Another Danger of Depression

In Step 6 I will talk more about alcohol, but I cannot leave the topic of depression without underscoring the problem of alcohol. As we all know, alcohol itself is a depressant. If you are serious about digging out of depression, you must avoid or seriously limit your alcohol consumption. That goes for marijuana use, as well. I see far too many patients who self-medicate with marijuana and do not accept the damage they are doing to themselves long-term. Marijuana use is far more common among middle-age professionals than many people realize. Alcohol, of course, is even more widely abused.

Gordon's Toxic Stress

My patient "Gordon" drank a six-pack of beer every night. His late-night drunkenness angered his wife, and they fought, and Gordon felt even more depressed about his marriage. His wife was struggling with depression of her own—postpartum after the birth of a child. The wife no longer could work, and finances were tight. I was concerned that Gordon had thought about suicide.

I learned that Gordon's greatest fear was that the stress might push him back to using cocaine, which his wife also feared. Alcohol was a starter drug to him. I told him he had to stop at one beer. "I can't do that. I need it after the stress of my day at the office." Yes, you can limit your drinking. You just have to value the benefit and embrace the goal. People like Gordon need to choose and schedule another stress reliever, such as exercise or meditation.

GORDON'S TOXIC STRESS

DIFFICULT LIFE SITUATION: Previous drug and alcohol problems; stressful work environment; overwork; a new baby; wife with postpartum depression
PHYSICAL DAMAGE: Gastrointestinal problems, weight gain, fatigue
DEPRESSION: Major depressive disorder, recurrent
ANXIETY: Generalized anxiety disorder (constant fear of slipping back into his lifestyle of cocaine and other drug use)
ACTION PLAN: Psychotherapy; relapse prevention and alcohol reduction; stress management techniques; referral to a psychiatrist for medications; scheduled exercise plan; couple therapy with contracted agreements for household chores and child care; and psychotherapy for wife to address her depression; AA support group
MEDICATION: Seroquel™ (antipsychotic), Wellbutrin® (antidepressant)

Summary

Depression, sometimes called the common cold of mental illness, is a core element in the toxic stress matrix. Mild depression responds to cognitive restructuring (correcting distorted thinking), behavior modification, light therapy, relaxation, diet and exercise, pet therapy, art and music therapy. For more serious cases, new medicines afford a jump-start on feeling better with very few side effects. Psychotherapy with a professional may be necessary. Though depressed people tend to deny themselves pleasure, healing depends on some forced re-introduction of pleasure.

In this step, you self-diagnosed the symptoms of depression.

Strategies and Techniques

Select those that will become part of your personal Action Plan to Recovery.

Seek professional help
- ❏ Talk to a doctor
- ❏ Make an appointment
- ❏ Consider medications (prescription or herbal)

❏ Assess yourself with the Beck Depression Inventory or other depression screening tests. How often? _____

❏ Bibliotherapy _____

Recognize distorted thinking
- ❏ Use cognitive restructuring When? _____
- ❏ Use the Triple-Column Technique to repair distorted thinking When? _____

❏ Create a Pleasure File Use when? _____

❏ Try art, music or dance therapy How often? _____

❏ Try light therapy How often? _____

❏ Pet therapy

❏ Reduce alcohol consumption and eliminate illegal drug use

❏ Join a support group

Step 3

Defeat Anxiety
and Anger

Step 3

Defeat Anxiety and Anger

Jana's Toxic Stress

"Jana" came to me after her supervisor discovered her curled up under her desk, having a panic attack, a severe form of anxiety. Jana's life was a mess. She had five children at home, including an infant, and a disabled, unemployed husband. She slept only two hours a night, took care of the kids, dealt with the bills, did all the shopping, food preparation, housework and laundry—and then she went to work for twelve hours on the night shift. There, the reality of her burdens closed in on her, and the panic attacks began.

JANA'S TOXIC STRESS

DIFFICULT LIFE SITUATION: History of childhood abuse; overwhelming family responsibilities; no support system, financial debt and conflicts with her primary family

PHYSICAL DAMAGE: Migraines, weakened immune system, frequent colds, overweight, disrupted sleep cycles

DEPRESSION: Major depressive episode

ANXIETY: Panic attacks

ACTION PLAN: Psychotherapy; marital therapy; problem-solving—negotiation with husband on sharing of duties, transfer to day shift and formulating a more structured approach to the management of the home environment; attempting to reduce stressors; assessing sleep patterns and creating a better sleep structure; relaxation techniques

MEDICATION: Zoloft® (antidepressant), Xanax® (antianxiety), Ambien® (sleep)

Panic attacks like Jana's are a form of anxiety. Anxiety is a core element in the toxic stress matrix. The feelings are of apprehension, fear of the future, fear of failure, fear of danger. This is the worry mode that will not go away and brings with it uncomfortable physiologic and emotional effects. Anxiety disorders are the most common of all mental health disorders. They are illnesses interwoven from a person's life experiences and in some cases genetics. They run in families.

Common forms of anxiety are:
Acute stress syndrome
Post-traumatic stress syndrome
Panic disorder
Obsessive-compulsive disorder
Generalized anxiety disorder
Social anxiety disorder
Agoraphobia and other phobias

Our Lesson in Terrorism

Terrorism at the World Trade Center will forever be an example in psychology because an entire nation witnessed it on television. We saw not only the physical events but also the panic of people running from it, ash-covered, bleeding, disbelieving. It is easy to understand how those people will suffer psychological problems for a long time to come. For many, the diagnoses were acute stress disorder and, later, post-traumatic stress disorder. These are medically defined varieties of anxiety that produce the same physical response as stress in general—the cortisol and adrenalin, the spiraling effects on the heart, lungs, digestive system and over all immune system.

In the World Trade Center example, the people on the streets of New York were not the only sufferers, however, because television brought the event into our homes. Research tells us that fifty percent of our learning is vicarious. We learned of the terror via television. Some of us processed that and over a relatively short time found a healthy perspective in which to regard those images and events. But people with depression or conflict or general stress already in their lives were more vulnerable. Some of my clients already in treatment for depression or anxiety told me they sat glued to their televisions for days. They identified with the tragedy. They experienced it, and re-experienced it, vicariously.

I diagnosed several of these patients as having acute stress disorder, as if they had been there themselves. They felt a numbing of their senses and capabilities, they could not sleep, they became hyper-vigilant, worrying when the next horror would come. Acute stress disorder lasts a minimum of two days and a maximum of four weeks, by definition in the DSM-IV—the *Diagnostic and Statistical Manual of Mental Disorders, Fourth Edition*—published by the American Psychiatric Association. This reference book details specific criteria that must be present for a diagnosis of various conditions. (An excerpt from the DSM-IV is included in the Appendix.)

In part, the DSM-IV defines acute stress disorder as diagnosis for a person who has

- experienced or witnessed an event that involved actual or threatened death, and
- responded with intense fear, helplessness or horror,
- recurrent and intrusive distressing recollections of the event, including images, thoughts, perceptions or dreams,
- physiological or psychological reactions,
- difficulty falling or staying asleep,
- significant impairment of social or workplace function.

Post-Traumatic Stress Disorder

The close of the Vietnam War brought post-traumatic stress disorder to the public's attention. Men and women who had experienced the guerilla war and its atrocities returned home but could not function in the workplace or in relationships. They had flashbacks, and lived too many hours of the day in anger, depression, drug and alcohol abuse.

From earlier designation as "shell shock" or "battle fatigue," the definition of post-traumatic stress disorder developed over the last quarter century. Post-traumatic stress now is defined as lasting more than one month. It usually shows up within three months of a traumatic event, but occasionally may not show up for years afterward. Recovery varies greatly from patient to patient and with treatment.

Post-Traumatic Stress Disorder and Domestic Violence

The single most common source of post-traumatic stress is domestic violence, for which the great majority of people experiencing it never receive treatment. As many as 4 million women may be physically abused by their husbands or live-in partners each year. Only a fraction of those are reported to law enforcement, and even fewer seek and receive psychological therapy. In ninety-two percent of all domestic violence incidents, crimes are committed by men against women, though reports of woman against man, same-sex domestic violence and elder abuse are increasing. You may be one of those numbers, or know of someone who is.

Other causes of post-traumatic stress are serious accidents or natural disaster such as earthquakes, or violent attacks such as rape, torture, mugging or kidnapping. Research shows that people with these events in their histories and with flashbacks in their present lives are especially vulnerable to ordinary stressors, such as the tailgater on the highway or the production quotas at work or the marriage partner making demands.

My patient "Cara" reported that she had been raped by a man she knew.

Cara's Toxic Stress

Cara's husband found her curled in the fetal position and distraught. She avoided his questions, but eventually she told him she had been raped by an acquaintance. Over her objections, he insisted that she report the rape to authorities. She did, though she could not remember much. After enduring the embarrassing questioning by police and treatment in the emergency room, she went home to try to recover from her trauma.

Several days later, she was shocked to find police officers at her door. They arrested Cara for filing a false police report. Not only had her rapist convinced them that he and Cara had had consensual sex, he had pushed them to file charges against Cara. He was a prominent businessman in the community.

The worst was yet to come, however. Cara's mug shot and her name appeared in the newspaper. And that is when Cara wound up in the hospital, and I was called in to help her.

She was deeply depressed and could barely respond to my questions. She was having frequent flashbacks. She was numb from the shock of her name and face in the newspaper. Certainly, Cara's situation was toxic stress and a whole lot more, but here are her elements.

CARA'S TOXIC STRESS

DIFFICULT LIFE SITUATION: The reported rape, the arrest, the article and other media attention

PHYSICAL DAMAGE: Hospitalization after attack, physical bruises, fibromyalgia, sleep disturbance

DEPRESSION: Major depressive episode, requiring aggressive medication treatment guided by a psychiatrist

ANXIETY: Acute stress and later post-traumatic stress, multiple flashbacks debilitating her in every way; dissociation; amnesia; anxiety and fears related to the reprisal by the perpetrator; panic attacks

ACTION PLAN: Psychotherapy that revealed marital and drinking problems; relaxation therapy; marital and family therapy; treatment of dissociative symptoms and amnesia; psychological testing with the MMPI-II (Minnesota Multiphasic Personality Inventory-II) and Beck Depression Inventory

MEDICATION: Flexeril® (muscle relaxant), Xanax® (antianxiety), Zoloft® (antidepressant)

BIBLIOTHERAPY: *The Dance of Anger: A Woman's Guide to Changing the Patterns of Intimate Relationships* (Lerner), *Control Your Depression* (Lewinsohn), *Lift Your Mood Now* (Preston)

Psychotherapy and Talk Therapy

Many, many research studies show that psychotherapy and talk therapy work. They can actually change the chemistry of the brain in the way that an antianxiety medication can. In psychotherapy, a psychologist or other therapist guides the patient to articulate and assess his symptoms, feelings and sources of stress, depression, anxiety or other condition. This exercise provides self-insight. Therapists typically help patients develop a treatment plan, which is similar to the Action Plan that this book advises. The treatment plan addresses such matters as symptom relief and, later, problem-solving.

Talk therapy can be viewed in two ways. One is the old model of psycho-analysis in which the patients tells and explores childhood issues in a Freudian model. Talk therapy can be just talk between friends and/or family. You share your problems, and your friend offers insight, perspective, support, maybe even advice. Above all, in psychotherapy and in talk therapy, there is a catharsis in-volved in "unloading" the burden verbally, letting someone else understand it.

A research study identified empathy as the most effective variable in psy-chotherapy. Empathy was more important a factor than anything else, including the gender of the therapist. And empathy is something that friends can provide.

Cara needed a lot of empathy. In our therapy sessions, a different picture of her horror emerged. Cara did not remember details of the rape she had re-ported because she was drunk, which the man she accused told police. He con-vinced them it was consensual sex, and Cara had no credibility to dispute it. Unquestionably, she was distraught over it. I provided a statement about her debilitating depression and anxiety, and her attorney arranged a plea bargain in which Cara paid a nominal fine in court for filing the false police report. She is now in AA, putting the rape behind her and working on her marriage.

SUPPORTIVE TALK THERAPY WITH A FRIEND

Choose a friend you can count on for empathy and insight.

Take your time together seriously, as part of your Action Plan.

Define your stressors, your "difficult life situation."

Define your physical health.

Define what you feel emotionally—depression, anxiety.

State your options as you see them.

Seek your friend's view of your options.

Conclude your talk therapy with one or two short-term goals.

Seek professional help if this does not help you to feel better.

Post-traumatic stress disorder (PTSD), as Cara had, is a debilitating condi-tion centered on flashbacks, or persistent frightening thoughts of the originating event. During a flashback, a person "tunes out" of the present and mentally reenacts the event. This can last seconds, minutes, hours, and, more rarely, days. People with PTSD relive the trauma in nightmares and/or disturbing thoughts during the day. Their moods are affected—becoming more irritable, aggressive or even violent. They may become depressed, feel detached from others, feel numb. They may be easily startled or have trouble sleeping.

In reacting to all this, people with PTSD sometimes compound their problems by turning to alcohol or drugs. They self-medicate to numb the emotional pain. They may not be able to function in the workplace or manage home life.

It sounds like a confusing mixture of symptoms and problems, and people experiencing PTSD may not realize that they are related. But they are, and many of us have experienced it or know people who have. The National Institute of Mental Health estimates that four percent of the population experiences symptoms of PTSD in a given year.

A New Therapy

Eye Movement Desensitization and Reprocessing (EMDR) is a relatively new therapy shown to be especially effective in treating post-traumatic stress. EMDR uses eye movements or other forms of rhythmical stimulation to stimulate the brain's information processing system. The repetition of moving the eye back and forth, or of tapping on your left side, then your right side while focusing on your past trauma seems to create a "disconnect" in the brain. So when you think of your trauma sometime in the future, you can view it less painfully.

I mention EMDR because it is an option for people with PTSD, and possibly other anxiety or depression. You would need to find a trained clinician who would use EMDR in combination with other therapy.

Generalized Anxiety Disorder

Another anxiety disorder that develops from stressors is generalized anxiety disorder (GAD). This is chronic, excessive worry preventing everyday function. People with GAD typically worry about a multitude of things, from relationships to finances to workplace. They may realize their worry is out of proportion, but they cannot control it. They are on edge, tense, irritable. They may have headaches or muscle tension. Depression, insomnia, light-headedness, excessive sweating—these are more symptoms. Women suffer from generalized anxiety more than men. If this kind of worry persists for more than six months, it is diagnosed as generalized anxiety and you should seek professional help.

Social Anxiety

Social anxiety is similar but driven by an insecurity of being in social or public situations. A person with social anxiety might dwell on how others are perceiving him, watching him or judging him. There is no way to relax or let down the defenses. Research studies found social anxiety to be the third most prevalent psychological disorder, behind depression and substance abuse.

Sasha's Toxic Stress

"Sasha" and her husband came to America from Russia. They had been here several years, and now in her late twenties Sasha was working full-time and trying to finish a college degree. Sasha's job was as a receptionist, but meeting people and dealing with strangers was her greatest fear. Sasha was sure that those people were watching her, even laughing at her. The woman was beautiful but she was sure other people judged her harshly.

She was struggling with the job when her professor presented her the biggest challenge ever. She had to do an oral presentation of her term project in the class. This was beyond butterflies over public speaking. Sasha was paralyzed with fear.

We worked it out, however. The professor gave her an extension so I could help her prepare. We did cognitive restructuring (correcting her distorted thinking) and cognitive behavioral rehearsal—practicing in my office how she would prepare herself mentally each step of the way through the presentation. With each step—such as setting up the Power Point program or taking her position in front of the class—I would ask her to assess her anxiety on a scale of 1 to 10. If her anxiety was high, we would work on ways to lessen it with deep breathing and relaxation techniques. We would correct her distorted thoughts and create a positive mental image to focus on, along with positive self-statements. Step by step, we made it through, and Sasha presented the best case study in that semester's class. Medications also helped.

SASHA'S TOXIC STRESS

DIFFICULT LIFE SITUATION: A traumatic childhood in Russia and loss of her family; dealing with people in work and social settings; intense social fears; background of verbal abuse as an overweight child
PHYSICAL DAMAGE: Migraine headaches
DEPRESSION: Dysthymia
ANXIETY: Social anxiety disorder and panic attacks
ACTION PLAN: Correcting distorted thinking and negative self-statements, cognitive rehearsal, relaxation techniques
MEDICATION: Paxil CR™ (antidepressant), Xanax® (antianxiety)
BIBLIOTHERAPY: *Help for Shy People* (Phillips), *Ten Days to Self-Esteem* (Burns), *Progressive Relaxation Training* (Bernstein and Borkovec)

When the Diagnosis Is Complex

Corrine's Toxic Stress

Corrine did not know what was wrong. Her heart would race, she could not breathe, and once when this happened, she blacked out. Corrine was so terrified of blacking out again that she would not drive, even to work. She was fearful of everything around her. For her first few visits to me, her husband not only had to drive her, but also had to coax her into the elevator for the ride up.

Corrine was having panic attacks, with agoraphobia—the fear of leaving home or other place of perceived safety. She also exhibited symptoms of an obsessive/compulsive disorder, the disorder known from the Jack Nicholson role in the film *As Good As It Gets.*

Corrine worked as a receptionist at a busy travel agency. At peak periods, customers formed long lines and focused their anger about their long waits on her. She was out there alone with people who were angry and threatening. She used to be able to handle it, but now she dreaded going to work and often called in sick because of her anxiety and panic.

Just understanding that it was a panic attack and that she was unlikely to die from it seemed to help Corrine. Medications and the identification of other problems in her life led to her recovery. In the meantime, she was still working at the travel agency, and she needed some better ways to cope. We used the Triple-Column Technique for correcting her distorted thinking, as explained in the previous chapter on depression—replacing a negative, irrational thought with a positive, more rational statement.

I also encouraged Corrine to use her natural wit. She had been the baby of her family and had made her mark as a cute, funny kid. She was a classic class clown. So when a customer would complain, she would draw upon some light sarcasm or poke fun at herself. She also developed a way to duck her head under the desk and make a very ugly face, venting the real feelings she might have about a difficult customer and thereby relieve some of the stress.

CORRINE'S TOXIC STRESS

DIFFICULT LIFE SITUATION: Dealing with angry customers, having no way to handle her stress and resolve their complaints; job dissatisfaction

PHYSICAL DAMAGE: Self-medicating stress symptoms with alcohol; migraines, jitteriness, trembling

DEPRESSION: Dysthymia

ANXIETY: Panic disorder with agoraphobia, obsessive/compulsive disorder

ACTION PLAN: Medications for anxiety; psychotherapy; relaxation therapy; use of antipanic techniques and stress management techniques; cognitive restructuring; controlled drinking; weight management; problem-solving that sent her to a vocational counselor for assistance in relocating to a new job and career counseling

MEDICATION: Ativan® (antianxiety), Xanax® (antianxiety), later changed to Topamax® (mood stabilizer)

BIBLIOTHERAPY: *Getting Them Sober* (Drews), *Hope and Help for Your Nerves* (Weekes), *Don't Panic: Taking Control of Anxiety Attacks* (Wilson)

HOW TO RESPOND TO A PANIC ATTACK
OR DIMINISH OTHER ANXIETY

1. Deep breathing; fill your lungs and release.
2. Positive affirmations: I am OK; this will pass; I know what it is.
3. Check your thinking; restructure negative thoughts.
4. Walk, jog, exercise.
5. Distract yourself—sing, dance, do housework or repair, count things.

In the more severe cases of anxiety, like Cara's and Corrine's, medication is essential. Typical antianxiety drugs include Ativan®, Klonopin®, BuSpar® and Xanax®.

How to Feel Better Today

The opposite of anxious and stressed-out is relaxed. So that is the relief you are seeking when your body is tense and the cortisol has shot through, spiraling its negative physical effects.

Relaxation therapy helped Corrine and Cara. For anyone living with toxic stress, relaxation is the "off" switch. Mind and body are transported to a zone in which the brain no longer recognizes the need for cortisol or adrenalin. The body gets its well-needed rest and you return to a state of calm or "homeostasis."

Relaxation Therapy

Relaxation breathing is a simple practice that takes ten to twenty minutes a day and can relieve the symptoms of stress—or anger, or anxiety. The technique was developed by Herbert Benson, M.D., at Harvard Medical School, tested extensively and presented in his book *The Relaxation Response*. I share an adaptation.

Relaxation Breathing

Preliminaries:

Select a quiet environment, the fewer distractions, the better.

Select a single-syllable word that you will repeat to keep your mind from wandering. PEACE, CALM, ONE.

1. Sit quietly in a comfortable position.
2. Close your eyes.
3. Deeply relax all your muscles (including the stomach, which should not be "in"). Begin at your feet and progress up to your face, concentrating on relaxing the muscles.
4. Breathe through your nose. Deep and slow. Become aware of your breathing. As you breathe out, say the word *peace*, or another word of your choosing, silently to yourself. For example, breathe IN ... OUT, PEACE, IN ... OUT, PEACE, etc. Breathe easily and naturally.
5. Continue for ten minutes, ignoring stray thoughts and concentrating on your word.

With practice, relaxation should come with little effort. Practice the technique once or twice daily.

Yogic Breathing

Anxiety commonly causes rapid, shallow breathing, a partner in crime with that rapid heartbeat. The antidote is deeper, slower breathing. Longer breaths get more oxygen to your brain and throughout your body. This is one of those good things. Your blood pressure should come down. Endorphins should flow, and you should feel better just by breathing.

In case you need instructions, though: Breathe through your nose slowly, deeply. Inflate the lungs fully. Yoga teaches, expand your belly. Without expanding your belly, you are not creating enough room for your lungs to inflate.

Exhale slowly, too. You may try exhaling through pursed lips so you can feel the volume go out. Suck in your belly to help push the air out.

That's it. Just repeat.

Breathing exercises are good strategies if you find difficulty in controlling your anger. Try incorporating anti-anger mantras such as "let it go," "take it easy," "this will pass."

One yoga breathing exercise that you may find therapeutic sounds quite strange, but feels quite good. It is alternate nostril breathing. Try this when stress is building—cut off the cortisol at the pass. I am not sure why this works, perhaps because you focus on the pattern of alternating, clearing your head of other thoughts.

Yogic Breathing Exercises

1. You can restore mental calm in one minute with "'alternate nostril breathing." Place your right thumb lightly on your right nostril and breathe in deeply through your left nostril. Close your left nostril with your middle finger as you release your right thumb and exhale through your right nostril. Do it again in reverse. In other words, switch to the opposite nostril each time you breathe out. Repeat the process for a minute.
2. Or try breath visualization. With your eyes closed, take in a deep breath, imagining it to be a beam of white, streaming into your body. Imagine it filling your lungs and sending out its white oxygen to your arms, your legs, your head. Exhale fully, and repeat.

Progressive Muscle Relaxation

An alternative relaxation practice is "progressive muscle relaxation," pioneered by Edmund Jacobson. You first tighten, then relax muscles, or groups of muscles, in a routine order—some people start at the feet, others with the arms. It is the routine that counts—eliminating your need to make decisions when you are trying to free yourself from responsibility. You tighten the muscle groups for five to eight seconds and then release. Imagine the stress flowing out of your body. Relax for fifteen to thirty seconds, then move on to the next muscle group.

As you learn what tenseness feels like, you will learn to relax your muscles at other times, as well—a good-health habit, kicking stress away.

PROGRESSIVE MUSCLE RELAXATION

Here's a sample routine, which should take fifteen to twenty minutes. In a quiet room sit in a chair with your legs uncrossed. Close your eyes to seal out any visual distractions. When you tighten a muscle, comprehend the tension, and when you release, appreciate how dramatically the muscle relaxes. Inhale while tensing, exhale while relaxing.

Once you become comfortable with this exercise, you may want to add a step—when you exhale in the release mode, say a cue word or phrase, such as *relax* or *trust in God* or *let it go*. Ultimately, your cue word will help you get to the relaxed state whenever you recognize muscle tension, which, of course, is a common physical symptom of stress.

1. Right foot — Stretch your toes backward.   Release.
2. Right calf — Lift your heel, pressing onto your toes.   Release.
3. Right thigh — Flex your thigh and squeeze your buttocks.   Release.
4. Left foot — Stretch your toes backward.   Release.
5. Left calf — Lift your heel, pressing onto your toes.   Release.
6. Left thigh — Flex your thigh and squeeze your buttocks.   Release.
7. Right hand and forearm — Make a fist.   Release.
8. Right upper arm — Bend your arm to show your muscle.
   Tense.   Release.
9. Left hand and forearm — Make a fist.   Release.
10. Left upper arm — Bend your arm to show your muscle.
    Tense.   Release.
11. Forehead — Lift your eyebrows.   Release.
12. Eyes and cheeks — Squeeze your eyes shut.   Release.
13. Mouth and jaw — Clench your teeth, grin and bare your teeth.
    Release.
14. Shoulders and neck — Lock your hands behind your neck.
    Press neck into hands.   Lift your shoulders.   Release.
15. Chest and back — Breathe in deeply, press your shoulder blades
    to the center of your back.   Hold the breath.   Release.
16. Abdomen — Suck in.   Release.

Contemplate your relaxed state.

Susan's Toxic Stress

"Susan" is a teenager in high school. Her mother brought her to me when she discovered that Susan was obsessively cutting herself. Oddly, this kind of self-wounding creates the same physiological response as other inflicted pain. Endorphins pour out and launch an anesthetizing effect. Susan was cutting herself because it made her feel good. She was acting out her anger in a way that relieved her stress.

The question for me was why would she be so desperate for those endorphins? The answer was that she was traumatized by her parents' vicious wrangling over their impending divorce. Their bickering and hatefulness caused Susan severe anxiety.

SUSAN'S TOXIC STRESS

DIFFICULT LIFE SITUATION: Dysfunctional family environment, conflicts related to her parents' divorce.

PHYSICAL DAMAGE: Self-mutilation, sleeplessness, agitation

DEPRESSION: Dysthymia

ANXIETY: Obsessive-compulsive disorder

ACTION PLAN: Psychotherapy; journaling; thought-stopping technique; exercise; problem-solving that led to relationship counseling with her mother and discussion about the pending divorce

MEDICATION: Zoloft® (antidepressant), Ambien® (sleep)

BIBLIOTHERAPY: *The Feeling Good Handbook* (Burns); *Between Parent and Teenager* (Ginott)

In a session with me, Susan gave her mother an ultimatum: Get the divorce, get it over. Her mother had been holding on to hope for a reconciliation. The fighting was a stall tactic, which Susan could see but the mother had not. Given the shocking damage the divorce had already done, the mother pledged to proceed with the divorce and to shield Susan from negotiations with her father.

Susan felt immediate relief and believed she could stop cutting, but we plotted a strategy for the future, just in case the parents slipped from their promises or another stressor came her way. Wanting to give Susan the same endorphins she felt when cutting, we chose jogging as a strategy. Whenever she would begin to feel anxious, Susan would visualize a mental picture of a STOP sign with running shoes on it. And then she would schedule herself a run and inform her mother of where and for how long.

CREATE YOUR OWN THOUGHT-STOPPING TECHNIQUE

Use the STOP sign as your palette and add to it an element such as running shoes or a smiley face or the person who loves you most.

Flash it mentally when you feel the first sign of stress or anxiety.

Then make time for a walk or relaxation or whatever technique works best for you.

Phobias

My patient "Crystal" suffered from a phobia, a kind of anxiety. In her case, the toxic stress was less of an issue, but I share her story to assure you that phobias are very treatable. Crystal was driving from the airport to her home late at night when she was rear-ended by a semitrailer. Crystal was seriously injured and spent several weeks in the hospital.

When she was able to walk again, she realized she was terrified of driving.

As we talked about that problem, I learned that Crystal's life was complicated by a difficult divorce and having to care for an elderly parent, and her own troubling diagnosis with multiple sclerosis. The driving phobia superimposed itself atop of all that, and Crystal was suffering severe toxic stress.

Together, we used systematic desensitization to address her phobia. This technique breaks down the cycle in which a person has trouble. For Crystal, we said she would begin preparing for a drive one hour ahead of time. She would do a relaxation technique. She would assess how anxious she was on a scale of 1 to 10. Next she would visualize getting into the car, and assess her anxiety on the 1-to-10 scale. She would mentally create a route or a roadmap and visualize arriving without harm or danger.

Breaking the process into small parts and visualizing success helped Crystal get back on the road. But only the back roads and side streets for awhile. She mapped out low-traffic routes before she drove so she could feel comfortable during the drive.

Crystal had one setback and became panicky. I asked what she was doing at the time; she had been distracted by listening to a talk radio show. I suggested buying a CD with relaxing, soothing music to play while driving, and it worked. When you are deep into anxiety, creative problem-solving sometimes requires the help of a therapist.

CRYSTAL'S TOXIC STRESS

DIFFICULT LIFE SITUATION: An auto accident, stressful divorce, continuous care of an elderly parent
PHYSICAL DAMAGE: Recent diagnosis of multiple sclerosis
DEPRESSION: Dysthymia
ANXIETY: Phobic reaction after a traumatizing event
ACTION PLAN: Systematic desensitization for her panic attacks (above); cognitive treatment for her depression; relaxation techniques for anxiety; problem-solving that referred her to support groups for education about multiple sclerosis
MEDICATION: Celexa™ (antidepressant), Xanax® (antianxiety)
BIBLIOTHERAPY: *Feeling Good: The New Mood Therapy* (Burns), *Progressive Relaxation Training* (Bernstein and Borkovec), *Hope and Help for Your Nerves* (Weekes)

Addressing Angry Emotions

Anger and anxiety produce the same physiologic responses, but anger is the ultimate in self-created stress.

Philip's Toxic Stress

"Philip's" girlfriend told him he had "an anger problem" and dumped him. "Don't come back until you deal with your anger," she said.

Philip didn't know he had an anger problem. He doted on the girlfriend, lavished expensive gifts upon her, took her to the best restaurants and resorts. What's this with anger? He came to me because he just didn't "get it."

Philip is a Type A, highly competitive and ambitious, very successful CEO in a high-stress corporate job. That is how he made the money he was spending on his girlfriend. The last straw for her was when they were traveling together and he wanted to upgrade to first class on a long flight. The airline agent explained that he could not do that, and Philip blew up, turning every head in the terminal to the scene.

Short-term, anger and aggressive behavior may bring results, as in competitive business. People give in so the angry person will calm down and end their discomfort. Not so with a personal relationship in which this girlfriend could just walk away. She had no children or complex finances in jeopardy, and she assessed that the expensive gifts did not outweigh the discomfort of living with a volcano awaiting the next reason to erupt.

When we looked at when and where Philip's anger manifested, we concluded that even business-wise, anger was not effective for Philip. He had high turnover among his staff of thirty. People do not enjoy a workplace steamed up with anger.

PHILIP'S TOXIC STRESS

DIFFICULT LIFE SITUATION: Girlfriend walked out; stressful work and competitive environment, failed marriage

PHYSICAL DAMAGE: High blood pressure, high cholesterol, tension headaches

DEPRESSION: Adjustment disorder with depressed and anxious moods

ANXIETY: Generalized anxiety disorder; highly Type A executive quick to anger, out of control

ACTION PLAN: Psychotherapy; referral to a neuropsychologist to further assess a diagnosis of attention deficit hyperactivity disorder (ADHD); anger management; assertiveness training; stress management techniques; cognitive behavioral rehearsal; visualization of successful performance in high-stress situations without losing control; problem-solving that helped him understand his girlfriend's need and how to maintain the relationship.

MEDICATION: Strattera® (ADHD)

BIBLIOTHERAPY: *Anger: How to Live With and Without It* (Ellis), *When Anger Hurts* (McKay and McKay), *Anger Kills* (Williams and Williams), *You Can Control Your Anger: 21 Ways to Do It* (Borcherdt)

We all experience anger. It is a normal emotion, and OK to have—unless your expression crosses the line and becomes destructive to you or others. The reason anger management is in a stress book is that anger is the ultimate self-created stress. You get mad, and you churn out the same stress hormones you might have needed for the saber-toothed tiger: adrenalin, or norepinephrine, and cortisol. Your heart beats faster, your blood pressure rises, you take shorter breaths and get less oxygen into your body.

That might be fine for slaying the tiger, but dealing with a difficult boss or the guy with "road rage" stamped on his forehead requires a more controlled response. And, as we have already established, you cannot live with toxic stress, or anger, without risking harm to your basic health.

Anger Management

Assessing your anger is the first step. What do you feel? Who or what triggers it? When do you lose control? How do you feel? Understanding anger and how to deal with it will put you more in control of your emotions and reactions. Self-diagnose your anger triggers.

SELF-DIAGNOSIS
My Anger
(Check those that apply)

Here are feelings that angry people often harbor.

_____ Anxious   _____ Frustrated   _____ Resentful

_____ Bitchy   _____ Hostile   _____ Numb

_____ Bitter   _____ Mean   _____ Sarcastic

_____ Depressed   _____ Paranoid   _____ Vengeful

_____ Destructive

Triggers: At whom am I angry, or with whom do I most often lose control of my anger?

_____ Myself   _____ My children   _____ All women

_____ My wife/husband/partner   _____ God   _____ Just in general

_____ My boss   _____ All men   _____ My past

Triggers: When and where am I most likely to lose control over my anger?

_____ Home   _____ On telephone

_____ Work   _____ In stores, restaurants

_____ While driving   _____ While traveling

What cues precede my loss of control over my anger?

_____ Muscles tense up   _____ Heart beats faster

_____ Voice changes (pitch, volume)   _____ Feel dizzy or confused

Other _____

With anger, you can coach yourself to a healthy, less-stressed response in three ways: (1) prevent it, or some of it, (2) control your arousal to it and (3) manage your response.

DEFUSING ANGER

Anger Prevention

Coach yourself to be alert to triggers and cues. Once you define your anger and what sets you off, you can mentally prepare yourself for situations in which you might get angry. Mentally coach yourself as if you were heading into the big game.

"Here's a situation in which I might get angry."

"I know who and what 'trigger' my anger, and I can watch for them."

"I know the 'cues' I get before losing control, and I can turn them off."

"I'm not going to take this personally."

"I will detach my ego and assess all statements unemotionally."

Develop your own inner pep talk of two or three statements that you can remember quickly and self-coach. _____
_____
_____

Anger Arousal

Coach yourself to turn off the physiological responses. When your cues kick in—your heart beats faster, maybe, and you know the adrenalin is starting to pump—slow things down. Anger and stress are identical at this moment.

1. Mentally coach your body to slow down. "Be calm." "Keep cool." "Take deep breaths."

2. Count backwards slowly from 20 to 0. This refocuses your attention to the numbers and away from the opportunity to express anger in counter-effective ways.

3. If time allows, use a muscle relaxation exercise.

4. Fast-forward your mind to a peaceful scene you have chosen in advance. Observe the details of your mental picture before re-entering the reality that sparked your feelings of anger.

Anger Management
Coach yourself to "hear" accurately and to communicate effectively. Mark Twain said, "If we were supposed to talk more than we listen, we would have two mouths and one ear." Before you react, be sure you have listened well. Analyze the situation honestly. Give other people the opportunity to express their side or view. You will be better equipped to present your side if you understand theirs.

The best way to handle anger is to express it in an assertive but not aggressive manner. Sometimes it's good to do that right away, clearly and without words that "bait."

- "I'm angry because the shipment you promised on Wednesday is three days late, and my customers are complaining."
- "I'm angry because my wife had an affair with her boss and I was the last to know."
- "I'm angry because I cannot make enough money for us to live as comfortably as we should."

In situations in which your physical safety is threatened or when the wrong response could jeopardize your job or family, for example, it's wise to suppress even your assertive response, or delay it.

Cognitive Behavioral Rehearsal

Armed with this perspective on triggers and responses, you can do as Phillip did—use cognitive behavioral rehearsal. Role-play the common scenarios in which you get angry and create more positive options for yourself. When you practice these scenarios, you train yourself to intervene before your anger causes you a problem. Sometimes I think of this as "reality therapy"—it is a small twist on cognitive restructuring. One key is to depersonalize the scenario.

For Phillip that meant telling himself that the airline was refusing to upgrade anyone who requested it, not just Phillip. He learned not to personalize situations. The whole system was screwed up if seats existed and could not be accessed. Sitting in coach wasn't so bad, actually, because he and his girlfriend had the middle seat between them if they needed more room. Phillip replayed this scene and others and began to understand how to turn down the burner on his responses.

Phillip continues to work at understanding the continuum along which assertiveness can quickly slip into aggressiveness.

Creating Your Own Calm

We sometimes forget that we really have choices in our lives. Sure, some of the most stressful situations are imposed upon us and our lives can seem out of our control. But if you look carefully, you will find opportunities to create your own calm, even if temporarily.

My patient "Abel" is an example of a person who had to create his own calm.

Abel's Toxic Stress

In the first week after the terrorist attacks on the United States in 2001, Abel came for a regular appointment. He had made excellent progress in coping with the stress brought on by divorce, a demanding girlfriend and children who needed his time and love. I expected this to be our last meeting. Instead, Abel walked in with an angry pace and body language. He was agitated, aggravated, highly stressed. I asked, "What's going on?"

He said he didn't know, he couldn't trace it. We reviewed past trouble spots and little by little we discovered that he had fallen off the program we had built together. He had lost the control over the external stressors in his life. He wasn't exercising, he wasn't using relaxation techniques, and he was letting his girlfriend take him away from his children, which made him feel guilty, resentful and angry.

I suspected that the newest stressor—the terrorist attack and loss of security—contributed to his fall from commitment to change his behaviors and take care of himself.

ABEL'S TOXIC STRESS

DIFFICULT LIFE SITUATION: Divorce—wife had left him for a string of other men; juggling the changed relationship with his children and the demands of a girlfriend and a work situation that was not satisfying

PHYSICAL DAMAGE: Overweight, gastrointestinal problems, high blood pressure, back pain

DEPRESSION: Major depressive disorder, recurrent

ANXIETY: Very anxious and agitated, couldn't sleep, couldn't function day-to-day at work

ACTION PLAN: Psychotherapy; anger management; reestablishing a schedule that included regular exercise and regular, nutritional meals; meditation; counseling on relationship building; return to medication prescribed by his psychiatrist

MEDICATION: Geodon® (antipsychotic), Zoloft® (antidepressant)

Abel was mostly angry that he was angry, and that he had lost control of his life. Divorce does that, all too often. Physiologically, Abel experienced the rush of adrenalin, the rapid heartbeat, high blood pressure—typical of anger, of stress, of anxiety. Relationship-wise, he was fighting with his girlfriend and his ex-wife. He was moody and not up to handling his time with the kids well. All in all, Abel was dysfunctional in the day-to-day routines of his work life.

Re-establishing a daily routine was critical to Abel's healing. We scheduled his days, hour by hour, to include regular meals, exercise, getting to work on time and meditative time for himself. Weekends were for the children. The girlfriend moved down on the priority list. The structure was a comfort to him, a calming force that required no heat-of-the-moment decision-making because the day was already lined out and he was committed to it. Abel and I also worked through some relationship building techniques that I share in the Love and Be Loved Step. His commitment to meditative time for himself brought great stress relief.

Meditation

Meditation is a form of conscious or chosen relaxation, and certain kinds of prayer can be, as well. Meditation in its simplest form is shutting out the thoughts that trouble you and, in fact, creating as blank a mental palette as possible. You sit comfortably, away from all distractions, and focus on your clear mind, your breathing, possibly a single word. It's all about focus, clearing out the mental clutter and chaos and honing in on simplicity.

Physiologically, meditation can turn off the cortisol. Research also shows that meditation slows the metabolism in red blood cells and suppresses the production of cytokines, proteins also associated with stress. Additional research shows how meditation can reduce hardening of the arteries, reduce blood pressure, heighten pain tolerance and improve mood.

Mindfulness Therapy

An alternative form of meditation is Mindfulness-based Stress Reduction. Research has been very positive on its calming effects. In the practice of mindfulness, you strive to stay in the present. You do not erase all the thoughts and images that occur, but you view them in a detached manner, nonjudgmentally. You notice detail but you do not engage your own emotions. For many people, mindfulness becomes a technique that they sometimes use when not meditating as a means of controlling the cortisol or anxiety in a stressful situation. The key is to detach. Meditation, therefore, is a kind of mental training.

All around the country, you can find programs that teach mindfulness. Most incorporate yoga, stretching or other light exercise, along with basic education on the physiology of stress.

There are many meditation techniques taught and practiced in Buddhism and associated with Hinduism. Certain yoga practices are meditative. I encourage patients who are intrigued to take courses, but most of my patients opt for the simplest forms or an adaptation of the Relaxation Response.

SUGGESTIONS FOR MEDITATION

Position, for basic forms: Sit in a comfortable chair or lie down.
Relax your body. Close your eyes.
Breathing, for most forms: Breathe deeply and evenly; inhale fully,
hold for five seconds; exhale fully,
hold for five seconds; repeat.
Time: Fifteen minutes is a healthful respite; you may want to build up to that.
Schedule your meditation for the same time daily.

Mantra Meditation

Choose a single word such as PEACE, ONE, LOVE, GOD, SHALOM.
You may say it aloud or just mentally express it. Repeat. Your mantra may
become a rescue word for you in times of stress. Just bringing it to your mind
may help you stave off stress.

Mindfulness Meditation

Your goal is to stay in the present. Keenly observe what you see, feel, smell,
taste. Make no judgments. Do not engage your emotions. If your thoughts
stray, bring them back to the present. Breathe deeply and regularly.

Other

The Relaxation Response developed by Dr. Herbert Benson, or my adaptation, is a proven technique.
Use guided meditation on a CD or tape, available at larger bookstores, to
assist you in achieving a relaxed state.

The Breath Prayer

The breath prayer is very much like meditation in that you focus only on its brief words. A breath prayer is short, personalized and easy to remember. A breath prayer has two parts—your name for the higher power in your life and your short statement of what you desire and need most. So you get:

Creator, grant me peace.
Gracious and loving God, fill me.
Lord Jesus, take away my anger.
My shepherd, protect me.
Father, let me feel thy presence.
Almighty God, make me strong.
Eternal light, envelop my children.

You may repeat your breath prayer slowly, perhaps once a minute, during a meditative ten minutes, or you may summon the breath prayer whenever you feel vulnerable. Like meditation, this kind of prayer drives out the frazzle of the rest of your life. Unlike the basic meditation described above, prayer provides not just stress relief but a greater measure of hope because of the underlying belief in a greater power.

The Serenity Prayer

Another short prayer appropriate for people living with toxic stress is the beginning passage of the "Serenity" prayer written by Christian theologian Reinhold Niebuhr. This prayer has been used for more than half a century in programs of Alcoholics Anonymous. This often-quoted passage from the prayer beseeches God for help in coping with change.

SERENITY

God, grant me the serenity
To accept the things I cannot change,
Courage to change the things I can,
And the wisdom to know the difference.

Other Therapeutic Forms of Relaxation

Massage

Massage is another relaxation option for people with anxiety, especially if muscle tension is present. If you cannot afford a professional massage, recruit a partner or do it yourself. You can use oil straight from the kitchen cabinet—sesame, sunflower or coconut are good. Pay special attention to your neck, shoulders, feet, hands and joints. An oil self-massage of the scalp feels great too. When you're finished, just shower off.

Research shows that massage therapy improves blood circulation, which can accelerate healing, increases endorphin production, relieves muscle tension and relieves insomnia in some cases. My former spouse and I were acquaintances of Bob Hope. Whenever we ran into him in our travels, he always had his massage table and sometimes his own masseuse traveling with him. He adamantly attributed his good health and longevity to a massage at the end of *every day.*

If you find yourself hunched over the computer too long at work, you can provide massage-like results with "tapping." A massage therapist recommended this to us. With a plastic water bottle or other similar object, tap the muscles at the base of your neck. Tap lightly ten to twenty times. It is an acupressure invitation for the muscles to relax.

Another at-your-desk technique is to take your shoes off and roll the soles of your feet over tennis balls. The eraser end of a pencil is another workplace object you can use as acupressure. Press the eraser into the palms of your hands, or at your temples.

Take time for yourself. Whatever works—do it on a regular basis.

Aromatherapy

Aromatherapy is still another tension outlet, and increasingly popular. Some patients enjoy it immensely, though take care if you are allergic to fragrances. Aromatherapy uses aromatic plant essences to invoke a sense of well being, calm and health.

Aromatherapy devotees add fragrance to the air and to the body. Add a few drops of essential oil to water in a diffuser dish, then light a candle beneath. Consider aromas such as lavender, lemon, rosemary, or whatever appeals to you. You can customize beauty products by adding a few drops of essential oils, too.

While aromatherapy seems rather superficially indulgent, some research shows it to be significantly comforting. At the prestigious Memorial Sloan-Kettering Cancer Center, patients exposed to a pleasant fragrance experienced sixty-three percent less anxiety while undergoing magnetic resonance imaging (MRI). Actually, a great deal of serious research has been done on fragrance affecting brain chemistry, sleep, creativity and sexual arousal.

Hydrotherapy

For centuries people have sought comfort from water, whether it be the Roman baths, the surf, mineral springs or luxury spa. If you are a "water person," a good soak can provide great relief from muscle tension. A warm bath or hot tub may also increase your circulation. While you are soaking, it is hard to remain angry or stressed out because your body is getting a physical comfort, which allows your mind to slow down. Hydrotherapy can be greatly restorative.

At luxury spas, you may take hydrotherapy in a private room with the tub in the center. The lights are turned off. You have a bottle of cool mineral water to sip. Aromatic bath salts give off a light scent. A computer-programmed cycle provides a variety of water and bubble intensity. Forceful jets of water massage your shoulders. Feet get special attention, and one cycle reminds me of champagne bubbles coming up the length of the tub. It is definitely a retreat from stress.

Summary

Anxiety, or unrelenting worry and fearfulness, is a core element of toxic stress. Identifying the kind of anxiety you are experiencing can help you problem-solve at its source and choose remedial techniques. Anxiety and anger present the same physiologic responses—an overload of stress hormones raises blood pressure, increases pulse, attacks the immune system. Muscle tension and migraines are common in people with various kinds of anxiety. Basic techniques of cognitive behavioral therapy can help you retrain your mind and body to halt or diminish anxiety and anger. Progressive muscle relaxation, yoga and breathing exercises also provide relief.

In this step you learned about anxiety disorders and self-diagnosed anger.

Strategies and Techniques

Check-select those that will become part of your Action Plan to Recovery.

❑ Self-assess your anxiety
❑ Seek psychotherapy with a mental health professional
❑ Practice panic attack responses
❑ Use breathing techniques to relax
   ❑ Relaxation breathing   How often? _____
   ❑ Deep breathing   How often? _____
   ❑ Yoga's alternate nostril breathing   How often? _____
❑ Use progressive muscle relaxation   How often? _____
❑ Use cognitive behavioral rehearsal
❑ Practice assertive responses
❑ Create your own thought-stopping technique
❑ Self-diagnose anger
❑ Self-coach for anger management   When? _____
❑ Meditation   When? _____
❑ Prayer   When? _____
❑ Use relaxation techniques. Choose a therapeutic form of relaxation.
   ❑ Massage   How often? _____
   ❑ Aromatherapy   When? _____
   ❑ Hydrotherapy   When? _____
❑ Bibliotherapy _____

Step 4

Think
with the
"Bright Side"
of Your Brain

If one advances confidently in the direction of his dreams, and endeavors to live the life
which he has imagined, he will meet with a success unexpected in common hours.
—Henry David Thoreau

Step 4

Think with the "Bright Side" of Your Brain

Marta's Toxic Stress

"Marta" had spent the first half of her life committed to being the best orthopedic surgeon she could possibly be. Long days of study and work became long years. Now in midlife, with no social life, with no meaningful relationship, she wondered about her choices. She had hidden herself in the demands of her surgical practice, but the truth was, she now was in burn-out. Professionally and personally, she had hit bottom. After a series of unsuccessful and unsatisfying relationships, she had become a recluse who holed up in the house on weekends, lacking the confidence in herself to function socially. It is hard to imagine someone with her talents unable to face the world outside her home and office, but that was the case.

Although she said she was ready to create a social life and participate in a relationship, she seemed incapable of beginning. We examined what she was thinking about herself, and what she was telling herself. We all engage in self-talk, and when we belittle ourselves, overcriticize, underestimate, all those negatives add up, and we begin to believe them. Examining Marta's personal self-statements, I could see that her negative self-talk denied her the self-confidence and self-esteem needed to attempt a new social life. Helping her recognize and correct the negative self-talk, distorted and irrational thoughts, was a challenge. If you are "thinking with the bright side," you will engage in loving self-talk, outlined as a strategy in this chapter.

Marta was highly motivated, however, and our sessions were fast-paced and charged with energy and ideas. We were able to proceed in the usual order of therapy—identifying the presenting problem, sorting out the core issues, establishing a therapeutic alliance between the two of us and crafting a treatment plan. This was the basis of hope for Marta.

Medications for depression and anxiety helped Marta to feel better, sleep more and enjoy a general sense of well being. She began to feel openly proud of accepting new social invitations as well as confronting and dealing with troublesome relationships in her past. Her self-esteem grew.

MARTA'S TOXIC STRESS

DIFFICULT LIFE SITUATION: Job burn-out, failed relationships
PHYSICAL DAMAGE: Migraines, complete burn-out, fatigue, sleeplessness
DEPRESSION: Major depressive disorder
ANXIETY: Social anxiety disorder requiring medication; some obsessive-compulsive traits in workaholism
ACTION PLAN: Psychotherapy, personal trainer for exercise, Pleasure File, problem-solving, accepting invitations to social events
MEDICATION: Lexapro™ (antidepressant), Xanax® (antianxiety), Ambien® (sleep), Travadon (antidepressant/sleep)

As you think about how your self-esteem and outlook compare to Marta's, here is a quick test for you.

1. Is your self-esteem high? Yes No
2. Are you a positive thinker? Yes No
3. Do you have a positive attitude toward life? Yes No
4. Are you an optimist? Yes No

If you said "yes" to all, your self-concept is solid. Any "no's" and you have work to do. This chapter will help you build self-esteem, which will help to diminish the stress you create for yourself with dark side, or negative thinking. You will learn how to:

1. Talk to yourself lovingly
2. See potential not problem
3. Visualize calm and success

Why Is Good Self-Esteem So Important?

Research shows that people with healthy self-esteem suffer less stress, depression and anxiety. One study from John Hopkins' Center for Health Promotion suggests that people with positive attitudes may produce fewer stress hormones, which in turn means greater protection from heart disease, which was the focus of that study. Therefore, if you want to feel less stress, think more positively about yourself and your circumstances.

Eleanor Roosevelt said it well: "No one can make you feel inferior without your permission."

Inferiority, now termed low self-esteem, is what many people feel when they cannot cope with the stressors in their lives, especially when they also struggle with anxiety or depression. Eleanor Roosevelt recognized that self-image is self-determined, and therefore completely in a person's reach to change it.

Ralph Waldo Emerson wrote, "A person becomes what he thinks about most of the time." Now we have the science to back them up.

It's a brain thing, and therefore a thinking, or cognitive, thing: You are what you think. You feel what you want.

You are what you think—are you the victim of stress or the manager of stress? Which do you want to be?

You feel what you want—your opinions shape your emotions. If your opinion of yourself is positive, you feel better. Therefore you can choose how you feel by altering your opinions, and here's the important part: by preaching them to yourself.

Talk to Yourself Lovingly

Many people living under stress can identify with self-criticism. They see themselves as unworthy, maybe even hopelessly flawed. You can pick your own negative label: stupid, ugly, incompetent, foolish, weak, abusive, cold, boring, lazy, procrastinating, flabby, sloppy, nasty; black sheep, goof-off, screw-up, slob, jerk, pushover, bully, liar. . . .

These labels you have for yourself, whether you say them out loud or not, may hold some truth, but most of us tend to exaggerate our weaknesses and underrate our strengths. Such mental self-poundings are potential self-fulfilling prophecies. At the very least, they are self-inflicted stress—reminders that you do not measure up to your own standards.

Research shows that self-talk, or automatic thought, begins about age two. The things you say to yourself are like tapes that get replayed and replayed. Unfortunately, most of us do not speak very kindly to ourselves on those replaying tapes. Research shows eight out of ten self-statements are negative. "That was a stupid thing to do." "I am a boring human being." "I hate my thighs."

When I coach golfers on the "mind game" of golf, I suggest that they test themselves on how frequently they engage in negative self-talk. Prior to a round I tell them to fill their right pocket with golf tees. They are to transfer a golf tee to their left pocket each time a negative thought or self-statement occurs. Back in the clubhouse, golfers are amazed at the number of tees in their left pockets.

Non-golfers may simply do a tally on a notepad through a day or two, or jot down circumstances and times. It's good to get a handle on how frequent your negative statements arise. Try to bring these automatic thoughts into your conscious thinking mind so that you can begin to recognize them and make the effort to change them to more positive ones.

Step 2 on depression explained how to identify distortions of facts, challenge them and rephrase them more fairly. Those principles apply when you are talking to yourself as well as to others.

One additional technique for improving your self-talk is to simply stop that negative thought, similar to the thought-stopping technique from the previous chapter. Choose a cue—a word or action that you will employ each time you hear negative self-talk. It could be as simple as the word *stop.* Or make a tight fist and release it—a physical signal to yourself. Then, of course, correct your negative talk, just as you correct other distorted thinking. Rephrase, reframe and give yourself a break. You do not have to lie to yourself about how great you are—but you really should look for your own strong suits and remind yourself of those. Think about how nice it feels when someone compliments you. That is the kindness you owe yourself in self-talk.

When your self-esteem seems low, make a list of your strengths and remind yourself of the personality characteristics that make you unique or special.

LOVING SELF-TALK EXAMPLES

I am smart enough to find the solution.

My children love me.

I struggle with my weight, but I can lose a pound a week, and that will add up.

My work is stressful, but I can use my two breaks for meditation or a walk, and I can get through the day.

I want to control my anger, and I can. I will count to three before I answer.

I can get organized and that will reduce my stress.

Recall a compliment a friend or colleague paid you and reaffirm your value and worth.

Daily Affirmations

These affirmations are from my friend and colleague Dr. Priscilla A. Marotta, who practices psychology in the Fort Lauderdale area. Priscilla included them in her own book, *Power and Wisdom: The New Path for Women.* They address common areas of self-doubt in women but can apply to men, as well. Use these, or use them as models for your own affirmations. I like the idea of affirmations on "sticky notes." Place them in different parts of your home and give yourself a little boost as you move from room to room.

ON ACCEPTING MISTAKES AS AFFIRMATIONS OF TRYING HARD

I will engage in self-correction, not self-condemnation.

Corrective input from others is to be welcomed nondefensively.

A mistake is an opportunity for new learning.

If there is a mistake, I will be gentle and tolerant with myself.

Mistakes are part of my humanity, and I refuse to condemn myself for any shortcomings or mistakes.

As a seeker of excellence, but not a perfectionist, I am open to direction and constructive criticism.

ON DEVELOPING CONFIDENCE BASED ON REAL CAPABILITIES

My relationships are only a portion of my life, and I am independently capable.

I can set meaningful goals that give direction to my life.

I can choose what I want and go after it.

I can ask for help when I need it.

I can be flexible and persistent in pursuing my goals.

I recognize and develop my talents.

ON THINKING POSITIVELY

Remember the wisdom of Eleanor Roosevelt: No one can make you feel inferior without your consent.

I am a worthwhile person.

I can do anything I set my mind to.

I recognize that my thoughts create my feelings.

I affirm myself daily.

I am the captain of my own cheerleading team.

I am committed to liking myself and accepting myself.

Attitude is important and my attitude is that I see the glass as half full.

See the Potential Not the Problem

In this, the second thrust of thinking on the bright side, ask yourself: Are you optimist or pessimist?

Research shows optimists are healthier in mind and body. They resist infectious illness and fend off chronic diseases of middle age better than pessimists. They are less likely to develop depression. Optimists even live longer and happier.

Optimism is also a predictor of high achievement in almost every field—from the golf course to the board room to the family home. If you can think it, you can be it!

Let optimism guide your life—think only positive thoughts. I have modeled the following advice from the timeless words of the Scottish novelist and poet Robert Louis Stevenson (1850–1894). He struggled to remain positive but understood its essential value. Together, we advise not just cognitive, but also lifestyle, choices that can help you achieve true optimism.

RULES OF THE OPTIMIST'S ROAD

1. Commit to being happy and finding pleasure.
   Martin Seligman of the University of Pennsylvania wrote *Learned Optimism: How to Change Your Mind and Your Life,* based on more than twenty years of clinical research. You can teach yourself optimism. Positive self-talk is an excellent beginning.

   Optimists do live longer—scientifically proven in research called the Nun Project, analyzing measurable optimism and longevity.
2. Laugh more than you cry.
   Humor really is the best medicine. Keep a book of jokes or cartoons by the bed. Something to make you smile! Research also shows that laughter lowers the levels of the stress hormone cortisol.
3. Do your best and be your biggest fan, not your biggest critic.
   Pay attention to the angel on your shoulder and not the devil. Sometimes criticism is petty, sometimes it's right on target. But once you have acted on it, push it out of your brain. Make room for the positives. Let your angel be your guide.

4. Be true to yourself and your values.

   When you examine the stressors in your life, do you find unrealistic expectations in the workplace or conflicting values in a personal relationship? When you understand your own values—and that may take focused introspection—you can sort out where conflicts exist. Conflicting values can produce high stress, especially in a marriage. Be true to the morals and values inculcated at an early age.

5. Stay out of debt.

   Love and money—when things go wrong, stress goes up. When money is a problem, make it a top priority to resolve. A quick fix followed by a long-term strategy is best for peace of mind and a less-stressed body. Create a budget or plan and live by those guidelines.

6. Don't borrow trouble.

   Avoid arguments over minor matters. Being less stressed is healthier than being right. Pick and choose your battles—you cannot win them all. You don't have to attend every argument you're invited to. Recognize distorted thinking, challenge it and correct it.

7. Don't carry a grudge. Cut some slack for people in your world.

   Hate, blame and gossip will sap your energy and spirit. Push them off your mental agenda to make room for pleasure and success. Replace blame with forgiveness and feel better for it. If you simply cannot forgive, let go. Picture all of your anger balled up in your fist, then release it like a butterfly. Picture it fluttering out of sight. Stress is your reaction to change. More often than not, you can choose how you react, and make the change more easily by willing it away.

8. Broaden your experiences. Have a hobby, travel, join and interact with others.

   Curiosity is a wonderful trait to cultivate. People with curiosity attract others to conversation and interaction.

   I use travel as my personal reward. When I return from a trip, the first thing I do is schedule the next one. It's my "carrot," a future reward that will make long days of work worth the effort. Consciously make an effort to engage in those pleasurable activities that make you feel good and give you a sense of well-being.

9. Don't wallow.

   Perfectionism is a stress-maker. Grant yourself a daily mistake. Forgive yourself and move on. Ask yourself, "What is the worse thing that can happen?" Imagine it and realize that you are not out of control. Things will work out for the best if you can "let go" and live in the present. Fill your brain with positives—inspirational message in print, audio or video; music, affirmations ("I can do it."). Remind yourself daily, "Keep it positive."

10. Give your talent and support to others who need it.

    When you embark on self-improvement, such as de-stressing your life, you focus on "me, me, me." Kindness to others, however, is rewarding, too. Take the moment also to experience gratitude for the good things in your own life. When you learn to give joyfully to others, you will find that you will get the same in return.

11. Show gratitude.

    Gratitude is the greatest of all virtues, Cicero said, and the parent of all others. When you are in toxic stress, seeing your blessings may be difficult. Recognize them, express them, act on them, however, and you will be amazed at the return on your investment. Gratitude can turn a negative into a positive.

12. Being thankful and give praise.

    Try setting a quota for yourself. "I will express my thankfulness three times today." Or, "I will praise my employees at least three times today." That puts you on the look-out for positives.

13. Prevent boredom with a variety of activities.

    Strive for balance in your scheduled life. Say "no" when you need to. But be sure to create relaxing time with friends and family and time for yourself. Allow yourself the time to do the things you truly enjoy. Commit to physical activity or exercise.

All this adds up to thinking with the "bright side" of the brain—planning to be optimistic, preparing to be positive and driving out any stray negatives.

Visualize Calm and Success

Visualization is the third major area in which you can improve your ability to "think on the bright side." Here's how legendary golfer Jack Nicklaus does it: "Before every shot, I go to the movies inside my head. Here is what I see. First, I see the ball where I want it to finish, nice and white and sitting up high on the bright green grass. Then, I see the ball going there, its path and trajectory and even its behavior on landing. The next scene shows me making the kind of swing that will turn the previous image into reality. These home movies are a key to my concentration and to my positive approach to every shot."

Jack Nicklaus is just one of many athletes who use imagery before competition. Imagery, or visualization, is a scientifically proven technique for improving sports or job performance, overcoming habits or behavior, and providing stress relief. With a mental road map of what you would like to achieve, you recall pieces of information and you shape those pieces into a mental video in which you achieve your goal. For Jack Nicklaus, maybe that's a birdie on the eighteenth hole. For you, it could be making the sales presentation to the new account, or telling the boss why you deserve a raise, or not yelling at the kids, or simply giving your body a break from the onslaught of stress hormones and stress symptoms such as muscle tension and headache.

The golf imagery story I most enjoy is of the Vietnam POW who survived his captivity by playing a round of golf in his head each day. He took great care to make the imaginary round as detailed as possible, actually walking the course in his head, noting his surroundings and closely focusing on each and every shot. After he was released and returned to health, he played the course he had rehearsed. He shot a 74!

Imagery is the ultimate form of "thinking with the bright side of the brain," whether in sports or in everyday life when you're coping with multiple stressors. Imagery, or visualization, can help you cope with stress in several ways:

- improving your concentration—by visualizing your success in the tasks ahead, you can prevent your mind from wandering when it is time to get the job done,
- building confidence—seeing yourself perform well in your mind makes you feel that you can be successful in action,
- controlling your emotions—picturing yourself in control will help you achieve control.

Generally, my advice is to use imagery in which you are the star player. But if the accomplishment is so far beyond your current expectation, start with a role model. Fifty percent of learning is vicarious. So watch in your head how your role model does it, then insert yourself. This works well with golfers who want to swing like Fred Couples or Tiger Woods, for example. They visualize his swing, then they mentally step in beside him and swing like Tiger or Fred. It's a matter of seeing and believing, and it pays off in results when you are on the golf course, or back in that stressful office. Visualize handling yourself well and gracefully dealing with every conflict that may come along.

HOW TO CREATE YOUR MENTAL VIDEO
A Guide to Effective Visualization

1. Choose a comfortable and quiet place to sit. No TV, no telephone, no other distraction.
2. Identify your goal—to succeed with a project at work, or to relieve tension, for example.
3. Relax. Imagery preceded by relaxation is more effective than imagery alone. Relax by using deep breathing, progressive muscle relaxation or relaxation breathing.
4. Close your eyes.
5. Imagine painting out all thoughts and images. Imagine filling your mental screen with one solid color.
6. Begin to create your scene. Fill in the background in as much detail as possible. If your goal is work-related, "see" the office in which you will work—the wall coverings, carpet, windows, lighting, chairs.
7. Add "sounds." What do you hear there? If you are visualizing a peaceful country scene, do you "hear" birds?
8. Add "smells" and "textures." Employ all the senses.
9. Put yourself in the scene. How are you dressed? What are you feeling?
10. "Walk yourself" through the process of achieving your goal. Savor your success.

Humor

Another way to protect your brain and body from stress is to have a good laugh. Think about how much better you feel when you have set aside your problems and spent an hour and a half watching a funny movie. When you come out of the theater, you feel a little euphoric, and it's because laughing at the humor in the film replaced the anxiety or depression—or toxic stress—in your life for that ninety minutes.

I would like to report that a wealth of scientific research supports the notion that humor heals and speeds mental health, but most of the research is on the benefits of laughter not humor. You can draw your own connection, of course. Norman Cousins wrote about how he laughed himself back to health in *Anatomy of an Illness,* published long ago but always a reminder of the effectiveness of laughter for some people. He spent many years at UCLA Medical School on humor-health research. Researchers at Loma Linda University in California also have published studies on laughter's benefits. According to the Association for Applied and Therapeutic Humor and other sources, research presents these conclusions.

- Laughter reduces cortisol.
- Laughter increases immunoglobin A, an antibody that helps fight upper respiratory disease.
- Laughter increases "natural killer cells" that fight viral-infected cells and some types of cancer.
- Laughter increases tolerance to pain.
- Laughter activates T cells that stimulate the protectivity of the immune system.
- Laughter increases heart rate and pulse rate temporarily.

Research does not—yet—prove that humor and laughter have definitive healing power. However, relieving stress and the damage that cortisol does to the body—whether by humor or other means—certainly improves health.

Have you ever heard of a laughter club? There is actually a Laughter Club Movement that began in India and wound up in the United States with a twist. Here, we view laughter as an exercise in health, so you find clubs meeting on the beach with "laugh leaders" taking them through routines that cause them to laugh. They practice their giggles, their titters, their guffaws. They do the conga line laugh, the roller-coaster-hands-over-the-head shriek, the knee-slapper. Everybody feels silly but better because of the physiologic changes that laughter brings.

There is some research that shows that induced laughter produces the same benefits as spontaneous laughter. In other words, you can laugh before you think something is funny and still feel better. You can fake it and feel better. This is good to know on those days when you are alone and feeling down. In the privacy of your home, you can just let out some big belly laughs, maybe even laugh at yourself for doing it, but rev up the endorphins.

If you have a naturally quick sense of humor, you have a great asset in combating your toxic stress. My patient "Christine" used hers to her advantage while working on a very serious problem in her marriage.

Christine's Toxic Stress

Christine is married to Jonathan, the former CEO of a large chain of stores in upstate New York. She had stayed at home to raise their children and to enjoy a quiet home life. She loved her home and spent many hours decorating and assuring that everything was in its place. He had worked long, fast-paced hours, overseeing twenty stores and more than 500 employees.

In the first year of his retirement, there still were loose ends to tie up in New York, so he traveled back and forth to their retirement home in Florida frequently. Then he came down for the whole "Season," generally Thanksgiving to Easter when the population in parts of Florida doubles with "snowbirds."

Without a company to direct, without employees to attend to his every need, Jonathan turned his attention to Christine, but in a negative way. He criticized her figure and her inability to lose weight. He nagged her to go on weeklong trips on their yacht, which she hated. He loved golf and tennis, she wouldn't play anymore. It was a very unhappy situation in which every day became an extended fight. The marriage was on the brink of divorce.

I worked with Christine, and then I worked with the couple together. They embody the value of hope and humor as you embark upon a course of change and recovery from toxic stress.

They latched onto the hope that we could save this marriage, and they used a humorous technique to reduce their fighting. They called it the Dollar Jar. We agreed that if either one of them felt the other had said something unkind, that offending person would have to pay a buck to the Dollar Jar. Because of Jonathan's competitive nature, he didn't like losing this game, so he reined in his temper. And she had official "permission" to stop the fight by saying, "Oh, that was unkind, Jonathan. You owe a dollar to the Dollar Jar." A fight of even a few minutes could become expensive.

The Dollar Jar was actually behavior modification that also created awareness of what each person felt was inappropriate, and therefore was educational. It was only a small part of their therapy, but it worked for Christine and Jonathan.

Christine's Toxic Stress

DIFFICULT LIFE SITUATION: A perfectionist dealing with new demands from her recently retired husband

PHYSICAL DAMAGE: Overweight, arthritis, migraine headaches

DEPRESSION: Dysthymia, negative attitude, low self-esteem

ANXIETY: Tension due to frequent verbal aggression

ACTION PLAN: Psychotherapy; exercise; marital therapy that led to mediated compromises on their lifestyle and the Dollar Jar

MEDICATION: Celexa™ (antidepressant)

BIBLIOTHERAPY: *Relationship Rescue* (McGraw), *Getting the Love You Want* (Hendrix)

Develop a Humor Inventory

Another way to use humor to de-stress is to be ready with a humor inventory. This is like the Pleasure File, but funnier. Make a list of the things you find funny: "The Three Stooges," Jay Leno, Archie comic books, reruns of TV sitcoms, knock-knock jokes, funny plays, Internet joke libraries, stand-up comedy, the Comedy Channel. You can find some comfort and security in knowing that you can select one of those activities when you need to break the cycle of toxic stress.

Appoint a Humor Ally

Do you have a friend who has a great sense of humor? Do you know someone who enjoys the same movie comedies that you do? That is the person to spend time with when you need a little humor or laughter in your life.

Here's how I helped "Melinda" relieve her toxic stress by redirecting her brain to picture something funny instead of the real-life boss who often launched into tirades, belittling her and putting her down. Whenever Melinda's boss yelled at her, I had Melinda mentally detach herself from the scene and imagine that instead of a ranting and rude boss she was watching a clown in full costume jumping up and down, waving his arms and grinning. The process distracted her from the emotion of the moment, and she could wait it out.

MELINDA'S TOXIC STRESS

DIFFICULT LIFE SITUATION: Working for a mean-spirited boss prone to temper tantrums; stressful life as a single parent

PHYSICAL DAMAGE: Recent surgery from a back injury

DEPRESSION: A major depressive episode; she was not sleeping and spent hours crying

ANXIETY: Generalized anxiety disorder

ACTION PLAN: Psychotherapy, relaxation tapes nightly, creative visualization, career counseling

MEDICATION: Lexapro™ (antidepressant), Sonata® (sleep)

The Smile

Closely related to humor therapy is smile therapy. Did you know that when you smile, you engage forty-seven muscles in your face? Did you know that when you smile you actually change the blood flow in your face? This causes the temperature of your blood to drop, and when cooler blood reaches the hypothalamus region of the brain, endorphins are released.

I would say that increasing the number of times you smile everyday is a no-brainer, but, in fact, it's very brain-centered. So make yourself smile. Stick smiley-face stickers on your mirror, your computer, your bathroom door. And be serious about smiling when you see them. You really will help yourself feel better.

Summary

Thinking with the bright side of your brain means being positive in all things, including how you think about and talk to yourself. Your self-esteem affects how you function in life, especially in interacting with other people. Optimism is healthy, and if you don't already have it, you can learn it. The mental video technique of preparing yourself for a difficult task will ward off stress. Prayer and meditation are ways to quiet the brain and turn off the stress hormones. And the old saying is right: "Laughter is the best medicine."

Strategies and Techniques

Check-select those that will become part of your personal Action Plan to Recovery.

❑ Practice loving self-talk
❑ Post and use daily affirmations
❑ Practice optimism   Specific goals? _____
❑ Post a reminder of any positive-thinking tips to be worked on
❑ Create a mental video   Situation? _____
❑ Humorous reading, music, movies   How often? _____
❑ Do a humor inventory
❑ Find a humor ally   Who? _____
❑ Smile more
❑ Bibliotherapy _____

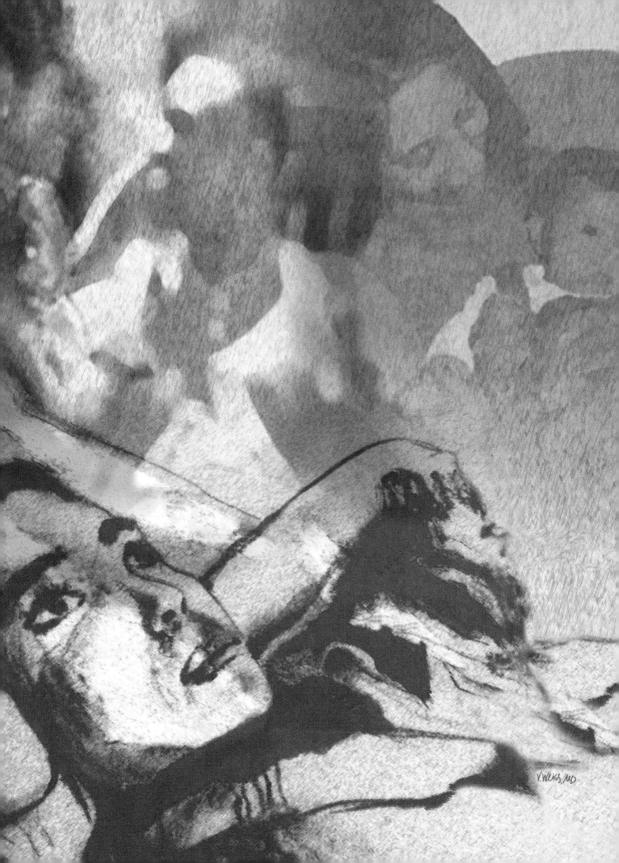

Step 5

Love
and Be
Loved

A true friend is someone who thinks that you are a good egg even though
he knows that you are slightly cracked.

—Bernard Meltzer

Step 5

Love and Be Loved

The Smiths' Toxic Stress

This couple and their six children felt the walls closing in. They had moved to a new town to join the family business, but their hopes did not pan out. The career change from academia to the dock and deck-building business was abrupt and not as lucrative as expected. Money was tight and the subject of many fights between husband and wife. The wife home-schooled their five children and was ready for a break from them at day's end. But when her husband pitched in, she criticized his every decision. The couple fought so viciously that there was little love left, and no sex.

For couples the Big Five of Stressors in a relationship, beginning with the most common, are (1) power and control issues, (2) the children, (3) money, (4) division of responsibilities and (5) sex. The Smiths had all five.

"To love and be loved" is advice for everyone—couples, adults, children, families, singles, heterosexual or gay. The power of giving love and feeling its force provides a safe ground, a security blanket of sorts, from which you can launch big and little change to solve problems and improve your life. If you are living with toxic stress, you need a lot of love from a parent, a child, a partner, a friend. Those relationships are life rafts on today's complicated seas.

THE SMITHS' TOXIC STRESS

DIFFICULT LIFE SITUATION: The move, career change, finances, child management problems, marital problems

PHYSICAL DAMAGE: Premenstrual Dysphoric Disorder, with intense mood and physical symptoms

DEPRESSION: Adjustment disorder with depressed and anxious moods

ANXIETY: Chronic anxiety over money, home-schooling five children; they fought incessantly over the children and money

ACTION PLAN: Marital therapy, communications skills training including "couch time," generating more intimacy in the marriage; child behavior management techniques; and problem-solving that utilized extended family for a support system

MEDICATION: Celexa™ (antidepressant)

BIBLIOTHERAPY: *A Couple's Guide to Communication* (Gottman et al.), *Intimate Connections* (Burns), *Living, Loving and Learning* (Buscaglia), *Between Parent and Child* (Ginott)

Love and Be Loved: Help for Yourself

It is the marriage relationship that most frequently gets entangled.

Mr. Smith came to me first, saying "I've had it." Divorce loomed, but I recognized a support system they had not yet tapped. A support system is the single most important factor for people under stress or, for that matter, for good mental health in general. The Smiths' extended family got together on Sundays, and when the Smiths ultimately shared their troubles, family members offered their support and love. The Smiths also had a church connection and a network of home-schooling families. And, finally, they had each other—if they could just get past the anger and fighting.

Sometimes we have to seek out the people who would be our support system and to ask for their help. To admit that you are in trouble, that you cannot cope, that stress is eating away at your physical and mental health—that's hard to do. It is embarrassing to admit vulnerability when our culture idolizes confidence and success. But turn to your support system and you will feel weight lifted from your shoulders, and with each lightening of the load you will be more capable of seeing solutions.

Vent to a Friend or Family Member

Venting to a friend reduces stress. Many research studies confirm this effect. It's like telling a tale to a bartender, but with less alcohol and more empathy. Validation and emotional support feel good. Explaining how you feel helps you label and identify elements of what is stressing you, which leads to better problem-solving. And, of course, two heads are better than one. A friend or relative can add perspective you might not have considered.

Support groups, especially those facilitated by mental health professionals, are excellent choices, too. Your local newspaper may list support groups, or ask the staff at a church or synagogue. When a person has no one else to talk to, that is when he or she winds up in my office.

Inventing a Support System

I grew up in a small town in New Jersey. Everyone knew everyone. I had aunts, uncles, cousins—no shortage of people looking out for me, no shortage of people to baby-sit when my parents went out or to buy me a Popsicle from the passing ice cream truck. As an adult, I moved away and had to create new support systems. We're a much more mobile society today, the divorce rate is high, and many people have to create new support systems several times in their lives. You might not know where to start.

I ask my patients, What gives you joy? Go there.

For me, it was golf. When I moved to Florida, newly single, I played golf and made friends who shared my passion for the sport. For other people needing to build a new support system, maybe it's volunteering at the hospital or sailing or a photography club. Seek out other people with like interests and find a way to hang out with them.

The Executive Women's Golf Association, founded in 1991, impresses me with its support-system concept expressed in its mission: "to foster a spirit of acceptance, dignity and respect for career-oriented women interested in golf." The network brings like-minded women together—and their golf games improve.

My coauthor, Patty Burnett, shares that her mother has belonged to the same bridge club since 1948 when the "Tuesday Bridge Girls" were young wives of Houston physicians embarking on their careers after World War II. They survived having teenagers in the 1960s together, and many other life passages.

I also escaped to a bridge group while raising my children. One or two nights a week our group of mothers played, often talking more about our problems than dealing the cards.

Isolating yourself is the worst thing you can do if you're strung out in toxic stress. You will feel better if you're connected to other people.

Make yourself connect. Even if you have to work hard to make it happen, like finding child care for your afternoon "off" from your stressors, do it. You will be turning off the stress hormones and giving your body a chance to recuperate from the onslaught.

TURN TO YOUR SUPPORT SYSTEM

Have lunch with a friend
Camp-out with another couple or family
Walk with a partner
Sign up for quilting classes
Attend Sunday School
Volunteer at the YMCA
Work with the PTA
Organize a potluck dinner club
Join, join, join!

- A sports league or club
- A support group
- A babysitting co-op
- A singles group
- A hiking club
- A motorcycle club
- An art class

- A service club—Rotary, Kiwanis, Optimists, Lions, AAUW, Knights of Columbus, Jaycees
- A Bible study
- A bridge club
- An exercise class

(Note: My coauthor Patty and I met when we joined the Rotary Club of Naples the same week.)

Love and Be Loved: Help for Couples

Loving and being loved are superior antidotes to stress, whatever its cause. A support system can provide that, be it family, friends or organized groups. If you are fortunate enough to have a loving and supportive partner, that takes the love infusion to a higher level. Think about the most loving couple you know. Do they cope well with stress? The saying is "love conquers all." At the very least, love trumps stress almost every time.

Loving couples can turn to each other for support. They are each other's built-in support group. Physical closeness helps, too. Research shows that hugs and affectionate touch reduce stress and depression, even boost the body's immune system. It follows that greater physical closeness can provide even greater comfort. Not all of us have that kind of relationship, however much we might aspire to. Nevertheless, it is helpful to look at what makes up that loving, anti-stress relationship so that we might grow into such a relationship or find some of its elements in friendship and other family.

The profile of a loving couple sounds a lot like the Boy Scout Law—trust-worthy, loyal, helpful, friendly, courteous, kind, obedient, cheerful, thrifty, brave, clean and reverent. In fact, many Scout teachings apply to relationships and stress management—do a good turn daily, be prepared, do your best, help other people, keep yourself physically strong, mentally awake and morally straight.

Janet Luhrs wrote the book *Simple Loving* in which she outlined twelve common characteristics of loving couples, as she observed from interviews of couples she admired. I really like what she concluded:

1. They have high levels of self-awareness.
2. They have a sense of purpose in the world.
3. They connect at their essence, rather than on the surface.
4. Something larger than the relationship keeps them together.
5. They are highly authentic, presenting their true selves to each other and to the world.
6. They are conscious and deliberate about the way they live their lives.
7. No matter what their income, they do not carry consumer debt.
8. They know what "enough" is for them.

9. They are able to see past the daily irritations to the big picture of their lives.
10. Their marriages are an evolution of two defined people who can stand on their own and yet be emotionally close.
11. They celebrate the simple pleasures of life.
12. They give more priority to their compassionate, open, cooperative loving souls, rather than to their outer, commercial layers of success.

The list indeed parallels the Scout credo.

"Family values" saved the Smiths. They asked for help from their church and their support systems, and they got it. Family commiserated and babysat, giving them a little time off from the stress hormones. Then we problem-solved their issues, one by one. For the Smiths, it was all about:

- Money—Once a month, on a Saturday when they are not stressed for time, the two of them sit down with the bills. They decide jointly on a plan to pay and save. Then the husband pays the bills.
- The children—The husband takes responsibility for the children from the time he gets home until their bedtime, and the wife agrees not to contest his decisions with the children during that time.
- Power and control—The plans for managing money and the kids were successful and encouraged the Smiths to try more planning and joint decision-making. They used a technique called "couch time" to declare a need for nonjudgmental discussion of problems that arose.

"Couch time" is uninterruptible, after-the-kids-go-to-bed, on-good-behavior time. The Smiths learned that the more specific they could be in advance about expectations, time frames and domains, the less likely they were to argue over an outcome. Couch time improves communication, problem-solving and organization.

If fights occur before you can get your couch time, declare a time-out and schedule discussion for the couch. Each partner must agree that when one declares a time-out, the other must respect it. This prevents destructive behavior and escalation.

- Division of responsibilities—Putting their expectations on paper helped the Smiths immensely.
- Sex—When the anger goes, when love returns, sex is not far behind. Bibliotherapy can help. One of my patients really liked *The Great American Sex Diet* by Laura Corn, a twenty-eight-day journey of sexy scenarios. Playfulness enriches your sex life.

The Smiths' story demonstrates the importance of problem-solving in recovery from toxic stress. Stress management techniques alone would only make them feel better. They had to get a break from at least some of the symptoms so they could use techniques like couch time and apply recommendations from books like *The Great American Sex Diet*. Effective, non-accusatory problem-solving ultimately would play a much bigger role in their lives than stress management. Problem-solving is the missing element in so many stress books that focus only on the temporary relief of physical symptoms. I hope the range of options and solutions you find in the problem-solving elements of my patient profiles will help you be equally creative and assertive in addressing the sources of stress in your life.

Three Wishes for Improving Your Life Together

Some couples live day in and day out in anger and never express what would make them happier. They just live in the criticism. I ask couples like that to each list three things that the other partner can do to make them more satisfied with the relationship. It's hard for them sometimes, and the answers are oftentimes surprising. The partner had no idea. This is a very simple exercise that can improve anyone's relationship, whether it's in trouble or not. You do something the other values, and he or she is grateful. It's a loving act.

Chad and Sue Ellen's Story

Chad is a physician's assistant. He and Sue Ellen recently had become parents to a son, who disrupted their lives more than they had expected. Chad was a neatnik, needing order in his environment. He hadn't wanted a baby in the first place, and now the baby brought the chaos of toys, special chairs and all kinds of gear, food and supplies. Sue Ellen had returned to work and could not keep up with the housework. The couple argued.

This was about division of responsibilities, and we found a quick solution in their "what would it take" lists. Every Sunday morning Sue Ellen would take the baby away from the home and have special one-on-one time with him. While she was away, Chad would power-clean the house and straighten the baby gear to his heart's content. As simple as this seems, this was an effective "what would it take." Everyone's happy.

I see relationship problems over the division of duties in all kinds of marriages, but they can get quite mean when two professional people go at it. It is division of duties/power and control all together. "What would it take?" works well in these situations.

Mystery Marriage Weekend

One of my patients came up with "mystery marriage weekend" as a means to demonstrate love and relieve stress at the same time. Man and wife were professional people with sufficient finances to indulge themselves occasionally. They agreed on how the mystery marriage weekend would work. When the husband saw that the wife was overworked or shouldering more stress than is healthy, he would send her a little love note telling her to mark a mystery marriage weekend on her calendar and save the date. He then would create a weekend trip that would delight her, making all the arrangements secretly. And she would do the same for him when she saw him getting in over his head. Maybe that would be a weekend trip to the baseball stadium and team he grew up with. Or for her, maybe that would be Broadway shows and dinner in New York. Everything would be scheduled and created for the other's pleasure.

Needless to say, the person on the receiving end was flattered by the thoughtfulness and thrilled with the experience. Surely there are less expensive ways to do this, too—a campout, picnic, candlelit dinner at home. As the saying goes, it's the thought that counts.

Assessing Your Own Relationship

Assessing your relationship's strengths and weaknesses is a good starting point for problem-solving. These are topics I discuss in premarital counseling, but they work for any relationship. You may think you know where your differences lie, but this exercise forces you to conceptualize better and scan the whole picture of your relationship. You can take the quiz together, or separately, then compare answers.

SELF-DIAGNOSIS
Our Relationship, For Better or Worse
(Circle the *a, b,* or *c* that best describes our relationship.)

1. Commitment and fidelity
    a. Marriage vows are the ultimate promise, never to be betrayed.
    b. Marriage is a legal agreement to facilitate social acceptance, melding of finances and parenting of children; people sometimes stray but can return to fidelity.
    c. Marriage is an unnecessary bond or one of which to beware, a step proven by the divorce rate to be flawed.
2. Trust
    a. I trust my partner totally to act in our mutual best interests.
    b. I trust my partner up to a point.
    c. I do not trust my partner to be honest and fair to me.
3. Lifestyle
    a. We share a common vision of how to balance work, family, individual interests, division of responsibilities, material purchases.
    b. We agree on most lifestyle issues such as balancing work and family, traditional versus nontraditional roles.
    c. We have differences on marital roles or on balancing individual preferences.
4. Parents and family
    a. We come from families with similar backgrounds and values—educationally, economically, career-based, religiously.
    b. We come from families with different backgrounds but common values.
    c. We come from very different families.

5. Children
    a. We share the same goals for having children or not having children.
    b. We haven't worked this out yet.
    c. We have very different ideas of family size.
6. Money
    a. We agree on matters regarding earning, spending and saving.
    b. We have some differences to work out still.
    c. We have different ideas about spending and saving.
7. Interests, hobbies
    a. We share many interests and appreciate others that our partner enjoys.
    b. We share some interests but have some that conflict with our partner's interests.
    c. We have very different interests in how to spend leisure time.
8. Personality
    a. We are alike in our personality styles and how we relate to other people.
    b. We are somewhat different in our styles but recognize and appreciate those differences in personality and approach to life.
    c. We are opposites or at the least different in our personality styles, which sometimes causes conflict.
9. Problem-solving
    a. We both are analytical but open to the other's ideas.
    b. Our approaches and ideas are different, but we usually work them out.
    c. One or both of us approaches problems with a tendency to criticize, blame or express anger.
10. Religion
    a. Our religious affiliation, or non-affiliation, is the same, and we seek the same level of religious observance in our lives.
    b. Our religious backgrounds are different, but we have worked out a mutual solution.

     c. Our religious backgrounds are different and can be a source of conflict.

11. Sex
    a. We are compatible in our level of interest, experience and sense of adventure in sexual intimacy.
    b. We have some differences but accept them and work to address them.
    c. We differ in our level of interest and/or the nature of our sexual intimacy, and this is a source of conflict or disappointment.

12. Power and control
    a. We agree on how we divide decision-making—either in a traditional marriage in which the husband takes the lead role, or in another arrangement.
    b. We play this by ear, and it works most of the time.
    c. We disagree frequently over how and when things are to be done, money to be spent and other issues.

Quite obviously, the more *a*'s you get, the better. Too many *c*'s and you have a relationship with some serious obstacles to fulfillment. A mix is a mix, to be considered by you subjectively.

Sex in the Marriage

Helen and Dave's Toxic Stress

For "Helen" and "Dave" their sex life was the central source of the tension and anger between them. He pressured her for frequent sex, but he experienced premature ejaculation and she was never satisfied. That, in turn, made her angry. This was a second marriage for both, but the husband was older and had very limited sexual experimentation, while the wife had experienced greater pleasure with previous partners. Stressfully, they lived day to day, knowing that he would ask and she would resist.

> ### HELEN AND DAVE'S TOXIC STRESS
>
> **DIFFICULT LIFE SITUATION:** Incompatible sexual needs and serious financial problems
>
> **PHYSICAL DAMAGE:** She was being treated for problems of menopause, their long conflict had worn her down, and the stress no doubt had affected her immune system. He had high blood pressure.
>
> **DEPRESSION:** Adjustment disorder with depressed and anxious moods
>
> **ANXIETY:** She was anxious and angry; he had performance anxiety problems that caused premature ejaculation
>
> **ACTION PLAN:** Marital therapy to restore sex, love, trust and respect; weekly "dates"; daily "niceness"; problem-solve sexual differences using Masters and Johnson's technique of "Sensate Focus" (a well-researched and effective technique)
>
> **MEDICATION:** For Helen, Lexapro™ (antidepressant); for Dave, Wellbutrin® (antidepressant with fewer side effects on sexual performance)
>
> **BIBLIOTHERAPY:** *Relationship Rescue* (McGraw), *The Pleasure Bond* (Masters and Johnson), *The Great American Sex Diet* (Corn)

Helen and Dave's problem was actually more about power and control than sex, but they did not understand that right away. Their initial goal in therapy would be to restore love, trust and respect.

They scheduled a regular date with each other, a baby step compared to mystery marriage weekend. They agreed to commit a daily niceness to each other, and they kept logs of the nice things the other said or did, which became reminders that there was a lot of love in their relationship. They wrote love notes to each other in a couple's journal.

Then I taught them a decision-making process that for them became the How to Resolve Our Conflicting Sexual Needs paradigm. It is a way for people to resolve differences without uncontrolled anger or emotion. There are rules, and each person must agree to them.

RULES OF ENGAGEMENT FOR COUPLES IN CONFLICT

1. You will meet at a scheduled time and place when you will have no disruptions.
2. The person with the problem speaks first.
3. The first person will define the problem from his or her point of view.
4. The other person will listen attentively not only to the words but to the feelings the speaker has about them.
5. The listener may not interrupt or react to what the speaker says.
6. When the speaker concludes, the listener will respond first with a "reflective I-statement" that recognizes what has been said and validates the anger, pain, consequences that the speaker has shown. "I can see you are really angry about ..." "I can see this has been very painful for you."
7. Then the responder has his turn to comment. "I really do see that you feel this way, however I feel ..."
8. After each person has had an opportunity to express opinions and feelings that help identify the problem, you may move on to brainstorming solutions. You will make a list of all possible choices. Do not judge them as you go. Simply list them. Think "outside the box."
9. Now prioritize the list, designating those that you agree are the most viable.
10. Using the technique of alternate speaking rights you will choose one to try for a set period of time.
11. If that solution does not work, you will go back to the list and select another.

By assuring fairness and a degree of civility The Rules of Engagement for Couples in Conflict remove some of the stress of negotiating a solution.

Communication 101

Do unto others as you would have them do unto you. You get what you give. Give and you will receive. Love begets love. Garbage in, garbage out. We know these truths, we sometimes just act like we don't. In any relationship both words and action are judged or perceived positively, neutrally or negatively. Take responsibility for your side of the exchange. Invest in the language of fairness, kindness, courtesy, civility, generosity, honesty, respect, trust and love, and you will be repaid.

WORDS TO STAY MARRIED BY

I love you	Please forgive me
I am so proud of you	Please
You look terrific	Thank you
Good point	What can I do to help?
Remember when ...	We are so blessed
I'm sorry	I cannot imagine being married
How are you feeling?	to anyone but you

SHOW YOUR LOVE

Do a daily "niceness" (good deed)
Keep a log of daily "nicenesses" done to you
Schedule a weekly date
Plan mystery marriage weekends
Say one nice thing to each other every day
Give a daily hug and kiss
Give gifts
Send cards
Draw hearts on sticky notes
Forgive

Stress-less Parenting Skills

Remember the Big Five of Stressors in a relationship? Number two was the children. "To love and be loved" is very hard when you fight over the children or when the children's behaviors add chaos to the home.

Mary Lee's Toxic Stress

"Mary Lee" had had a heart attack. She was only fifty-two years old. Her doctor said stress caused her heart attack, and she had better learn to deal with stress or she would be back with another heart attack.

By nature, Mary Lee was a worrier, and her life provided plenty of opportunity. She worked for an insurance company, managing a large department, budget and staff. At home, she raised a daughter who challenged her in every way—school performance, drugs, and pregnancy at age sixteen. She went on to have three children by three different fathers. Two of the children lived with Mary Lee.

The oldest—eleven years old—had pulled a knife on the family and wound up in juvenile court. Adorable in all other ways, he was disturbed, and we put him into treatment. Mary Lee needed to understand why the grandchildren were so bad, and how she could help, while at the same time dealing with her own stress.

For Mary Lee, we determined that the highest-stress times were after school and into evening. Because the children were failing in school, Mary Lee had cracked down and required them to do their homework before they could play in the afternoon. It was a hard battle.

The boys told me that what they really wanted to do after being cooped up in school all day was to get outside, run around and play. The boys previously had been diagnosed as having ADHD; they were hyperactive.

We negotiated a deal. The boys could play outside until Mary Lee came home, around 5:30. Then they had to come in and do chores before dinner. Mary Lee also had to establish a more complete household schedule. The boys needed more structure to replace the chaos. It sounds like such a little thing, but their playtime deal and a set schedule for play, chores, homework and dinner changed this home environment. Mary Lee was the most amazed, and thrilled, of all.

The boys have to help with dinner preparation, and they agreed to that in exchange for that early play time. Everyone in the home sits down to dinner at 6:30. After dinner there is an hour of quiet time in the house, during which no radio, stereo, TV or phone can be used. This is homework time. If there's no homework, it's still quiet time.

I also shared with Mary Lee my philosophy about disciplining children. Punishment is ineffective. Think instead of "consequences" and "restitution." Instead of taking away a privilege such as playing outdoors before dinner, add something. If the child fails to do his chores, add a chore, maybe cleaning the cat litter box, or some other unappealing task. If you can tailor the consequence to become a learning experience, that's even better. Use discipline to teach behavior and values. When the child makes restitution by completing the added chore, you have the opportunity to praise him for a good job—further reinforcing positive participation in family life.

For Mary Lee, this behavior management technique also was a de-stressor.

MARY LEE'S TOXIC STRESS

DIFFICULT LIFE SITUATION: Raising difficult grandchildren

PHYSICAL DAMAGE: A heart attack, high blood pressure

DEPRESSION: Moderate depression

ANXIETY: Anxiety and worry about the chaos of the home and fear of how the children would turn out

ACTION PLAN: Behavior modification for her grandchildren, including family schedule and consequence-based discipline; diet and exercise for Mary Lee

MEDICATION: Zoloft® (antidepressant), Ativan® (antianxiety), Ambien® (sleep)

BIBLIOTHERAPY: *Changing Families* (Fassler et al.), *Parenting, A Skills Manual* (Guerney)

When determining consequences for children, here are a few tips.

- Define expectations and consequences in advance.
- Make them age-appropriate—expect more from a twelve-year-old than a five-year-old.
- Look for ways for the consequence to be a learning experience.
- Encourage older children to participate in choosing consequences or "retribution" options.
- Create a range of consequences for minor to major infractions.

My patient "Claudine" was at wit's end with her thirteen-year-old son "John." They were in a vicious circle of bad behavior partially fueled by John's Attention Deficit Disorder. When he would get angry and yell at his mother, she would ground him—taking away a privilege rather than adding a consequence. Grounding John meant he had no way to release his energy, and that is why I say it was a vicious circle. He got angrier and angrier, once even threatening to get a gun and start shooting. John would be grounded for two weeks, make a mistake, blow his top and be grounded again almost immediately. Grounding was not working.

For John, we used a "restitution list." He and his mother worked out the restitutions together. If he did not meet a basic expectation, such as returning home on time or controlling his temper, he would select a restitution from a list of ten they posted on the refrigerator. Cleaning the garage, raking leaves, washing windows—mostly things requiring physical energy (a help with the ADD) but that also relieved his mother of some of her stressors. She was raising three children virtually alone because her husband worked nights and rarely saw them.

As testimony to how stress affects the whole family, Claudine had been worried about her four-year-old and had taken her to their primary care physician. The little girl had been having severe headaches. Her doctor determined that the headaches were caused by the high level of conflict in the family.

Here is still another family story. The "Jensens" got a wake-up call when one of their two teenage daughters attempted suicide to escape the anger and conflict in their home. Both girls had been getting into trouble, and the parents fought over how to discipline them. The father's modus operandi was to abdicate communication until he was so fed up he exploded with anger. The mother tended to withdraw and let things happen as they might. There's a saying, the enemy divided has no power. The teenagers were getting away with a lot of irresponsible and disrespectful behavior.

Through therapy, the couple realized that some of their problems stemmed from their polar opposite personality types and neatness needs. He was authoritarian, though he imposed his demands only in angry outbursts. He was furious about the ongoing dishevelment of the house and one daughter's disastrous room in particular because as a child he had always been required to have a shipshape room. The wife was disinclined to set and police limits for her daughters. She also was a workaholic who enjoyed her professional life and had little interest in domestic duty such as house-cleaning.

When their daughter attempted suicide, they realized they had to become the team they had never been, despite their different styles and interests. They used the Rules of Engagement for Couples in Conflict to problem-solve, and these are some of their conclusions.

- A weekly family meeting—They chose Saturdays for a family brunch in which issues could be aired. The Jensens actually used Roberts Rules of Order to conduct these meetings. The meetings were highly instrumental in changing the environment in that household.
- The father, drawing on his organized, technical orientation, created a chart on which household chores and other agreed-upon tasks would be assigned and checked off.
- The wife created a reward system in which the daughter with the messy room received a monetary payment for accomplishing her cleanup. And this worked wonderfully for them, because money was a true motivator for the girl.
- They gave away the dog for which no one would take responsibility.

All three of these families—Mary Lee's, Claudine's and the Jensens—were living with conflict and chaos and benefited greatly from initial behavior and stress management followed by cooperative problem-solving and improved communication skills—where you take charge of your life and whittle down the chaos, anger, hurt, burdens and pressure.

Divorce Has a Price

I see many children of divorce. They lose a parent and lose a family. They see their parents fight before the divorce, through the divorce and then after over custody, visitation, rules and money. They are devastated, highly stressed. That is why so many courts, like Florida's, require families to complete a divorce education program before a decree will be granted. Parents learn how vulnerable the children are and how they can lessen the damage through cooperation and non-threatening communication. The children also get instruction, explaining that they are not to blame for their parents' divorce and showing them how the future can work.

Except in cases of abuse or criminality, I try to save the marriage. Divorce destroys dreams as well as families and finances. People lose years of their lives in just getting back to Square One. We also know that married people

- live longer: One study showed that men and women who experienced divorce some time in their life had a forty percent greater risk of premature death than those who were steadily married. Those who did not re-marry were 120 percent more likely to face earlier death.
- Achieve better health and wealth
- Experience more physical pleasure and emotional satisfaction from sex
- Suffer less alcoholism, depression and other mental disorders when compared to unmarried, divorced and separated people
- Are 3.4 times more likely to be happy than cohabitating couples
- Cope with stress and loneliness better

Affairs and the Damage They Do

The one kind of love you do not want is extramarital. Sixty percent of marriages end in divorce, and infidelity causes sixty-five percent of the breakups. You could even argue that stress causes much of the infidelity.

In her book *Make Up, Don't Break Up,* Dr. Bonnie Eaker Weil wrote, "There is a correlation between the many men who engage in extramarital affairs and the level of stress in their households."

In other words, men escape from the stress at home and fall into bed with someone with whom—at the beginning, at least—there is no stress. Dr. Weil believes it is because men feel the physiological distress that comes from confrontation or conflict in the marriage. "Men flee this discomfort to attempt to relieve, self-medicate and soothe the physical effects that conflict produces in them."

She believes that several factors lead to infidelity by men, also including unresolved emotional issues from childhood, adultery in the "family tree" and the same kind of brain-chemistry change of some early childhood trauma that the latest research casts as increased vulnerability to stress. Thus they cheat because of the stress.

Stress Threatens Marriage

To be fair, women cheat on their husbands too, increasingly. Weil's research suggests that seventy percent of men cheat on their spouses, as do fifty percent of women. My patient "Heather" cheated on her husband with another married man, inflicting relationship damage all around but also illuminating a major deficiency in her marriage.

Heather's Toxic Stress

Heather's boss made a pass and she accepted. Soon they were making wild passionate love behind closed office doors. The sex astonished Heather, who had never reached orgasm with her husband of fifteen years. With her new lover, she sometimes had five orgasms.

When her lover's wife made a surprise visit to the office, the affair and Heather's orgasms were over. She continued to work for her former lover, however, and you can imagine the stress in the office. Heather felt a great loss, she withdrew further from her husband, and she hoped therapy could help her decide whether to leave her husband and seek a new life that would include the intimacy she had experienced with the lover.

After addressing her depression, we embarked on sex therapy—coaching her to be more assertive in sex with her husband. She began to ask for things that pleased her and show her husband what she wanted.

When another man propositioned her, however, Heather succumbed to curiosity that he might be a better mate than her husband and equal to or better at sex than the first lover. I share this to illustrate why sex ranks as one of the Big Five Stressors in married life, and how it can be a deal-breaker. Therefore, when one partner isn't happy with sex, it behooves the couple to make some changes in their sex life.

The latest on Heather is that she is back to marriage monogamy, but her boss began another office affair and flaunted it to make her jealous. Our problem-solving on that led to this plan. Each time she felt angry or jealous, she would flash a mental picture of a hot sexual moment with her husband. She would plot the evening's activity. Worked for Heather.

HEATHER'S TOXIC STRESS

DIFFICULT LIFE SITUATION: Extramarital affairs, sexual dissatisfaction in marriage, jealousy, ineffective at work

PHYSICAL DAMAGE: PMS, weight gain

DEPRESSION: Major depressive disorder (wasn't sleeping, had no appetite or energy, cried a lot)

ANXIETY: Over how to cope and whether to end marriage; social anxiety, tension, irritability

ACTION PLAN: Psychotherapy; treatment for depression and anxiety; sex therapy; massage therapy; exercise and weight management; visualization

MEDICATION: Paxil CR™ (antidepressant), Ambien® (sleep)

BIBLIOTHERAPY: *Intimate Connections* (Burns), *Love Is Never Enough* (Beck), *For Each Other: Sharing Sexual Intimacy* (Barbach), *The New Joy of Sex* (Comfort), *Relationship Rescue* (McGraw)

Forgiving

Especially in cases of adultery, my patients tell me they can forgive but cannot forget. And I tell them they must find a way to forget, or to move on. Otherwise, the resentment lingers, they obsess and they still hurt.

What I find works best is to probe for psychic restitution. Here are three patient stories and how we problem-solved to arrive at psychic restitution. These happen to be dollar-based restitution—that is what eased the minds of these women.

"Geneva" had had it with her husband's affairs. This was the third of which she knew. She caught them in the bedroom at their beach house, so there was no doubt. Geneva was livid, but we found what would make it right for her. When she had married the guy, she had signed a prenuptial agreement that would guarantee her a modest income if they were to divorce. Her husband was fabulously wealthy, however. Geneva said she could "forgive" and let go if her husband would modify the agreement to guarantee her a $1 million lump sum and $75,000 a year income, for life, if he had another affair and she left him. The husband signed and was grateful that he could make restitution and have a happy marriage again.

"Belinda" had three small children that she left under the care of a nanny/housekeeper every day while she went off to work. Her husband worked from a home office, but apparently not full-time, because the nanny eventually confessed to Belinda that she had been having an affair with her husband.

Belinda could not purge the anger she felt toward him, yet she wished for a normal and secure family life for her children and for herself. We did the "what would it take?" exercise. The answer was that Belinda would become an equal partner in her husband's business—legally recorded. There would be no doubt about what share of the business she was due if he ever strayed again.

My third patient seeking appropriate restitution, "Sarah," named her price in carats—three in a marquis diamond ring.

Love and Be Loved: Help for Singles

Dating is a trial-and-error experience that you begin as a teenager. Most of us mature and date into our early twenties, or later, and most of us can recall moments in which we told ourselves, "I'll never do that again." Never get hurt or never date a person with an addiction or never date someone from work, and on and on.

Some of the painful learning is unavoidable. We are on a path to find the right person, and unless we are extremely fortunate, we have to weed out some "wrongs." It helps to create some basic ground rules that take in your experience and the wisdom of others. For women, I highly recommend *The Surrendered*

Single: A Practical Guide to Attracting and Marrying the Man Who's Right for You by Laura Doyle.

Some suggestions are in the accompanying box. Establish your own rules before you date and stick to them. It's much easier to say you have a "personal rule" than to ad lib a "no" on the spot. These tips are drawn from many sources.

BE SMART ABOUT DATING

1. Wait to have sex until you are in a relationship.
2. Consider it a relationship when you have dated at least six times.
3. If you have children under the age of eighteen, do your dating privately until you are sure of an ongoing relationship.
4. After a divorce, wait. You need at least a year. Do an "autopsy" on the relationship so you are clear about what went wrong and don't make the same mistake again.
5. Don't consider marriage until you have dated at least six months.
6. Be honest and know your partner through open communication.
7. Don't date people who
   Have addictions (the odds are against you)
   Are negative
   Are married
   Abuse you or others physically, emotionally or verbally
   Are self-centered and selfish
   Are controlling, manipulative or possessive
   Differ with you about whether to have children
   Break the law
8. Beware of the difficulties of dating people who
   Come from extremely different family backgrounds
   Practice a different religion
   Have a different educational and/or intellectual level
9. Date people who
   Share your values
   Share your religion
   Share or appreciate your interests

Share your views about having children
Share your feelings about family in general
Share your views on marriage
Share your views on money
Are at your intellectual level
Demonstrate their love and respect for you
Show and express affection
Share your needs for sexual intimacy
Tell the truth
And are kind and generous

10. Be careful about your vulnerability if you have recently lost a spouse or partner. Do not jump into another relationship too quickly.

Needless to say, love and hard work can overcome many obstacles in a committed relationship, but there are red flags that any dating person should acknowledge. When the red flag grows from a background flutter to one wildly waving in front of your eyes, it is time to cut your losses and move on. This is one of the hardest decisions for a single person—to realize that the relationship will not lead to the desired future and therefore must end. The decision gets even harder if you have lived together without marriage and have spent enough time with each other to own property, develop a circle of friends, attach to the extended families and, worse case, have children.

Living Together

Research shows that fifty percent of all contemporary couples who marry today cohabitated first. Public opinion accepts living-together arrangements as a trial period in which a couple can determine if they are suited for marriage. Yet research also demonstrates that couples who cohabitated before marriage are more likely to be divorced than couples who did not.

If you live together, don't kid yourself about the future. About forty percent of all cohabitating couples break up without getting married. There is very little in cohabitation that prepares you for commitment that is "through sickness and through health," good times and bad, ours not mine. Cohabitating is much more about dividing space than sharing it.

Cyber-Dating

I cannot discuss dating without mentioning the Internet. The Internet is singles central, and there is a slight connection to stress. For some reason, typing personal information on a computer screen is less stressful than having a friend "set you up." There's certainly an easier "out." You just stop typing.

I am not an expert on cyber-dating, but I am citing four highly stressed patients who have shared their stories with me, and every week I hear another Internet tale. However, I am told frequent stories of positive relationships and happy endings.

Miller's Toxic Stress

This is a short one. "Miller" had a rocky marriage. He had cheated on his wife, but he thought he had her calmed down. That was right up to the day she told him she had been having cyber-sex with a great guy from Texas and walked out. Cyber-revenge led to toxic stress.

MILLER'S TOXIC STRESS

DIFFICULT LIFE SITUATION: Divorce—devastated by his wife leaving him

PHYSICAL DAMAGE: Back problems from a running injury that kept him from jogging, accident-prone because he couldn't focus

DEPRESSION: Major depressive disorder

ANXIETY: Severe anxiety, not functioning at work

ACTION PLAN: Psychotherapy, cognitive restructuring, exercise, work on understanding relationships

MEDICATION: Paxil CR™ (antidepressant)

BIBLIOTHERAPY: *Rebuilding: When Your Relationship Ends* (Fisher), *Intimate Connections* (Burns), *Living, Loving and Learning* (Buscaglia)

Miller comes from a very conservative family background and had ingrained beliefs about traditional relationships. He was very hard on himself for his own failing, but his wife's actions shocked him. We worked hard on correcting Miller's distorted thinking.

Harry's Story

"Harry" had lived with a woman for several years when she talked him into getting married. Within six months, he knew it was a mistake. As a married woman, not just a roommate, she wanted control. Theirs was another power and control conflict.

Harry worked with me, and then we brought his wife into therapy. She was furious, very, very hostile over his cold feet and not letting her have her way. We could not save this marriage, though I worked privately with the wife for more than a year longer, helping her deal with her anger.

Harry came back to me, too. The ink wasn't even dry on the separation agreement when Harry started surfing the net for a new girlfriend. Whatever he shared in his profile—good-looking, independent businessman, likes to travel—it attracted women. At one point, his personal ad drew 600 hits a day.

The problem was that Harry doubted his ability to choose. He had not seen the trouble coming with his most recent wife, and he had three failed marriages before that. So Harry would cull a list of five or six, and bring the profiles to me. We would sort through and talk about the pros and cons, and potential hidden agendas, personality clashes and psychological baggage each might bring to a relationship.

We narrowed the list to two, and he traveled out of state to meet one. Though she had lied about where she really lived, which is not a good start to a relationship, this woman snagged Harry. They fell in love at the storybook first sight. She turned out to be a very wealthy woman with homes in two states, one in Manhattan. After only a month, they were talking marriage but Harry is still being cautious about another permanent commitment.

Cecile's Story

"Cecile" tells another side of cyber-dating. She and her husband both worked high-stress jobs and came home at night to two toddlers who needed much love and attention. Life was work, responsibility, laundry, cooking, home repair, financial issues—short on peace. The husband left.

I worked with Cecile as the divorce proceeded. At night when the kids were finally asleep, she hit the computer and entered the world of Internet dating. What she found was five or six guys who said all the right things on the Internet and telephone, but really weren't looking for companionship or a relationship, just sex. Still, she persevered and now feels more positively about the Internet as a means to find dateable men with common interests and values.

From both these patient stories, I think you can draw several conclusions:

- The stress of divorce—and the depression that often accompanies it as you grieve for your loss, the marriage—tears apart your self-confidence and self-esteem. Your judgment in the year following a divorce truly might be impaired.
- Just as in any dating situation, you must watch for the red flags, such as misrepresentation or outright lying. Some people write better than they behave.
- Personal safety is an obvious concern. In other situations, you date someone with connections at work or among friends, and you likely would at least know if the person had a criminal record. But the Internet protects no one.

Another patient, "Jackie," whom you will read more about in the next chapter, went from one bad relationship to another. While recovering from being rejected by a man she thought wanted a lifelong partner, she turned to the Internet. She was just days away from quitting her job and moving to New York to be with her wonderful new soul mate when she discovered he not only had lied to her about his prestigious credentials as a medical researcher in the Bahamas, but he had led on as many as thirty other women just like her into sexual relationships.

Beware the liars out there.

Love and Be Loved: Help for Gays and Lesbians

Gays and lesbians face all of the relationship issues that straight people do, and then some, because there is less clarity about the roles and expectations than, for example, in a traditional heterosexual marriage. This creates an insecurity, which feeds stress.

My patients "Ella" and "Jeneen" did not have toxic stress, but they did have a serious relationship problem that caused Ella to feel jealous and anxious. While Ella was working nights, Jeneen liked to visit friends' houses and bars and party late into the night. She is a pretty, flirtatious young woman. Sometimes when Ella came home from her night shift, Jeneen hadn't even made it back home. And this caused Ella's anger, insecurity, jealousy and deep hurt.

Ella and Jeneen had to negotiate and compromise on what each could live with, and they came to me to help them do that.

Jerry's Toxic Stress

I had another gay patient, "Jerry," who was single and struggled with the uncertainties of gay dating. Because of sexual dysfunction, Jerry had been seeing a urologist. The urologist, finding no physical source of the dysfunction, referred Jerry to me. Through psychotherapy, I discovered that Jerry was experiencing performance anxiety. He was sick of being picked up in bars by men who wanted only sex. Jerry's response was toxic stress.

JERRY'S TOXIC STRESS
DIFFICULT LIFE SITUATION: Gay dating scene, AIDS threat
PHYSICAL DAMAGE: Sexual dysfunction
DEPRESSION: Dysthymia
ANXIETY: Performance anxiety in an environment of expected promiscuity; panic disorder; obsessive-compulsive tendencies
ACTION PLAN: Psychotherapy treatment for performance anxiety and problem-solving that helped him clarify his own values; identifying personality characteristics of a suitable partner and developing a dating plan with new avenues for meeting prospective partners
MEDICATION: Wellbutrin® (antidepressant), Viagra®

Summary

Love and being loved are superior antidotes to stress, but love is not always perfect in itself. Little things like venting to a friend can help you gain perspective on relationship problems. Having friends and being a part of a group relieve stress and can be a source of empathy and insight when you need it. The five big stressors in a relationship are (1) power and control issues, (2) children, (3) money, (4) division of responsibilities, and (5) sex. Any can lead to toxic stress and your need to problem-solve. For singles, the guidelines of smart dating can steer you from the pitfalls. Beware, especially, of the danger of cyber-dating. Finally, gay relationships may take even more effort to succeed and for the benefits of loving and being loved to diminish stress.

In this step you self-diagnosed your relationship.

Strategies and Techniques

Check-select those that will become part of your Action Plan to Recovery.

Make connections

❏ Turn to your support system   Who? _____

❏ Vent to a friend or family member   Who? _____
When? _____

❏ Join, join, join   What? _____
Frequency of participation? _____

Show love

❏ Choose from tips such as a daily niceness
I will show love by _____

❏ Arrange a Mystery Marriage Weekend   How often? _____

❏ Practice Rules of Engagement for Couples in Conflict
When to use? _____

❏ Set aside "Couch Time"   When to use? _____

❏ Agree to use time-outs

❏ Define your "Three Wishes" for improving your life together

_____

_____

_____

❏ Commit to "Words to Stay Married By"
❏ Forgive
❏ Spell out your Psychic Restitution—What Would It Take?

_____

Improve parenting
    ❏ Use behavior modification for the children
    ❏ Use consequences not punishment
    How? _____
❏ Be smart about dating. My rules are:

_____

_____

_____

❏ Bibliotherapy _____

V. Wus, MD

Step 6

Commit to Health and Wellness

I find, by experience, that the mind and the body are more than married, for they are most intimately united; and when one suffers, the other sympathizes.

—Lord Chesterfield

Step 6

Commit to Health and Wellness

Jackie's Toxic Stress

"Jackie" came from a poor family but worked her way through school and parlayed her math skills into an accounting position. Newly divorced, she fell for Phil, a very wealthy retiree. He wined and dined her, lavishing attention and introducing her to his many friends at the country club. There was talk of them moving in together, and Phil and Jackie went house-shopping.

But one day, Jackie made a big mistake. She mentioned the M-word, marriage, and Phil dropped her flat—not a date, not a call after that. Jackie was devastated. She had no idea that Phil was unhappy with their relationship or disinclined to commitment. She began to have headaches, she could not sleep, and by the time she came to see me, she was experiencing major depression.

Jackie's treatment was multi-pronged, but exercise played a huge role. She hit the gym and worked out every single day for an hour to an hour and a half. She felt better, and she looked better, which made her feel even better.

Exercise is the No. 1 anti-stressor. With moderate exercise, you can turn off the stress hormones and turn on the ones that make you feel better and happier. You get:

- less cortisol (and reduced food craving)
- more epinephrine (and coping ability)
- more serotonin (and better mood)
- more dopamine (and better sleeping)
- more endorphins (and that great feeling)

For Jackie, working out released the anger and hate she felt for the guy who dumped her. She also required medications because the depression was severe, and we worked in session to help her gain a more realistic perspective of who this man was. We used cognitive restructuring to correct her distorted thinking, and in the problem-solving phase she chose to talk to other women who had dated this man. She concluded that he was a womanizer who had a pattern of passionate involvement with women followed by unexplained abandonment.

In the short term, Jackie got a grip, and from the gym she had a body to die for.

Jackie's Toxic Stress

Difficult life situation: Being rejected by a man she thought was leading her to the altar
Physical damage: Headaches, sleeplessness
Depression: Major depressive disorder
Anxiety: Anger and distress over her future and her misjudgment of Phil
Action plan: Psychotherapy including instruction in cognitive restructuring; daily exercise and attention to her physical health; problem-solving that led her to understand that the boyfriend had a pattern of treating women this way.
Medication: Zoloft® (antidepressant)

The New Endorphin Debate

Exercise improves your mood; that we know. Science is still working out the details of why. New research calls into question the widely held belief that endorphins released during exercise are responsible for the relaxed and satisfied feelings that follow. Endorphins seem to kick in only after strenuous exercise of forty-five minutes or longer. Now researchers are looking at norepinephrine as the key player. They think regular exercise may stimulate this neurotransmitter and directly improve the body's ability to respond to stress. Thus the person who exercises regularly gets a double benefit—immediately feeling happier and more relaxed after exercise and, long term, being better equipped to handle new stressors.

What Kind, How Much?

A combination of exercise is best, for many reasons. You are less likely to get bored and quit if you have variety. And while you're doing it for stress, you might as well reap the other important physiological and psychological aspects of exercise—protecting your heart, maintaining or reducing your weight, and making you feel better.

The American Heart Association advises you to include both aerobic and strength-training in your exercise regimen. The American Cancer Society recommends that you become more physically active by including at least moderate activity for thirty minutes or more on most days of the week. The federal government's Institute of Medicine shocked the country in 2002 by doubling the previously recommended amount of exercise, from thirty to sixty minutes daily. Do not let that intimidate you into doing nothing because you cannot do sixty minutes. Some is always better than none.

There is no shortage of advice, but the best is Nike's: "Just do it."

A SAMPLE EXERCISE PROGRAM

The American College of Sports Medicine recommends this program for a healthy adult.

Cardiovascular Training

Frequency—3 to 5 days per week
Intensity—low to moderate intensity, 60–85 percent of maximum heart rate
Duration—20 to 30 minutes of continuous activity
Mode of activity—continuous, rhythmical aerobic using large muscle groups (walking, jogging, cycling, swimming, rowing, in-line skating, stair-climbing, aerobic dance and cross-country skiing)

It is important to increase the amount of time and intensity of your exercise gradually. When beginning an exercise program, 5 to 10 minutes of activity may be all that you can do. Increase no more than 2 minutes per week.

Resistance Training

Frequency—2 to 3 days per week with at least one day of rest between workouts; do not do resistance training on consecutive days

Sets—a minimum of one set, 8 to 12 repetitions to near muscle fatigue

Number of exercises—a minimum of 8 to 10 exercises involving the major muscle groups

Speed—moderate to slow; each repetition should be approximately seven seconds

Range of motion—Exercises should be performed through a full range of motion and should be pain-free

Flexibility Exercises

Flexibility exercises (stretching) should be included with every exercise session. Before stretching, warm up with 5 to 10 minutes of light cycling, walking, rowing, etc. Each stretch should be held for 15 to 30 seconds and repeated 3 to 5 times, alternating sides. Do not stretch to the point of pain.

For people in stress, and for all of us who need ongoing motivation to exercise, I recommend a schedule. In my own life, I attend a strength-training class twice a week with a personal friend, Olea Defore, and aerobics or Pilates® class once a week. I take Sundays off, but on the other three days, I walk outdoors or on the treadmill for thirty to forty-five minutes.

I also appreciate the insight of fitness expert Denise Austin, who apparently has heard numerous excuses for why people cannot find time to exercise. On her web page she advises, "There's one main difference between people who exercise regularly and those who don't: Regular exercisers make their workouts a priority. If you have a busy schedule, you may want to exercise first thing in the morning. The blow-off potential only grows as the clock ticks and you become engrossed in the day's activities."

As I have always advised my busy son, it is easy to find an excuse, but make a commitment to your own health and well-being. This is especially important advice for those who work in stressful jobs or homes.

Walking

Walking is a great anti-stress mode of exercise, climate permitting. It is well documented—you get outside in the natural light, observe the world around you, the sky, the earth, other people's lives. Stride away from your stressors and detach from them. There is more to life than the stressors inhabiting your life.

Walking with a partner is doubly therapeutic. You get built-in commitment to the effort, plus there is an opportunity to share thoughts, even to vent.

WALKING, THE CHEAP ROUTE TO FITNESS
Walking has many benefits. It can:

- Reduce stress
- Encourage reflection or meditation
- Strengthen your heart and lungs and improve circulation
- Help prevent heart attacks and strokes
- Reduce your blood pressure
- Boost your metabolism
- Lower your cholesterol
- Tone your legs and abdomen
- Use calories and control weight
- Reduce arthritis pain, strengthen bones

Alcohol

When I say commit to health and wellness, I have to talk about the threat alcohol poses. People in stress often think their relief is in the bottle; you've heard it already in many of my patient stories. Indeed, alcohol relaxes—it sedates some brain function. The problem is that one drink can lead to two to four to five, and we all recognize the hazards to health and happiness. Alcohol added to stress or depression can compound your problems.

Alcohol actually stimulates the secretion of adrenalin, which is that stress-rush hormone. It can contribute to nervous tension, irritability and insomnia—none of them good for a person doing stress damage control.

The 12-Step Program of Alcoholics Anonymous is America's first choice of treatment. It is based on the belief that alcoholism is a disease, that people with this disease cannot control their drinking and must abstain entirely, that they can achieve life-long sobriety only through the help of a greater power, God. AA works for millions of people. It has saved many, many lives, and therefore has a passionate membership who believe that AA and total abstinence are the only answer for an alcoholic. AA is the prevailing treatment for alcoholism in the United States, England and some other northern European nations. Even the most elite alcoholism treatment programs, such as the Betty Ford Center, offer AA's 12-Step Program.

However, AA may not be the *only* answer for everyone. I have used controlled drinking for some patients. Many patients in the early stages of denial refuse to accept that drinking may be a problem for them. But they will agree that they need to manage and control their drinking more satisfactorily. Management of a drinking habit is a far more accepted choice of treatment in Canada and Australia. The basic concept behind this approach is that drinking lies on a continuum of use, abuse and dependence. With treatment, some—certainly not all—people can return to moderation.

In the final chapter of this book I share a decision-making model called Decisional Balancing, and I use changing your use of alcohol as an example. Generally, this is a means for you to analyze the pros and cons of changing your alcohol use. Drinking has consequences, some beneficial and some definitely not. Analysis of your drinking consequences is a first step for someone who wants to change, whether that change is total abstinence or controlled drinking. I like the comparison of alcohol use and dieting. If you blow your diet one day, you can declare yourself a failure and give up, or you can forgive yourself and start again.

Some people can make such changes without AA, without medications or other treatment. When they are asked how they did it, they said they just "thought about it" and made a commitment. They weighed the pros and cons, perhaps using the Decisional Balancing model.

That's not to say that change was easy. I read once that resolving an alcohol or drug problem was like hiking up a bumpy path. You want to reach the top, but there are dips, bumps and curves. Do not write off your chance for reaching the top just because one of those bumps in the path causes you to miss your goal of reducing or stopping your drinking. Drinking habits develop over a period of time and, generally, it takes time to change a major habit such as drinking.

SELF-DIAGNOSIS

Alcohol Consumption
THINGS TO THINK ABOUT WHEN DRINKING IS A PROBLEM

How I feel when I drink
    My emotional state (angry, abusive, depressed, happy, sad, bored)
        Before I drink
        After I drink
        What do I accomplish when I drink?
        What does it do for me?
    My physical state (relaxed, tense, tired, "wired")
        Before I drink
        After I drink
        Blackouts
        Memory loss
Where I drink
    At home
    In bars or restaurants
    At sporting events
    In friends' homes
When I drink
    After work
    After dinner
    Mornings or afternoons

With whom I drink
    Alone
    With others
    With others who also drink too much

Social pressure to drink in excess
    Do my friends also drink too much?

Consequences of drinking in excess
    Toll on my body
    Mood changes
    Others' reactions to me
    Legal problems
    Financial problems
    Work or school problems

Availability of alcohol
    Easily accessible?
Amount of time I engage in drinking

WRITE IT DOWN

1. Describe your most serious drinking situation.
2. Describe the factors (from above) that triggered that problem.
3. Describe the consequences, immediate and delayed, negative and positive, if any.

Repeat the exercise with another serious drinking episode.

KEYS TO CHANGING YOUR NEGATIVE DRINKING BEHAVIOR

    Identify the triggers and consequences.

    Develop alternatives to drinking activity.

    Plan how not to drink or over-drink.

    Recruit support from friends and family.

    Include this in your Action Plan to Recovery from toxic stress.

SUGGESTIONS FOR DRINKING LESS

Plan some alcohol-free days each week.

Drink no more than 12 drinks in a week.

Drink no more than one drink per hour.

Choose beer and wine with lower alcohol contents.

Dilute drinks with mixer or club soda.

Limit drinking to two per day.

In my practice I sometimes use hypnosis to help patients wishing to exercise moderation or abstinence. You could also try self-hypnosis.

Also, for people in stress, sometimes understanding the entire dynamic of stress, depression and alcohol motivates them to try behavior modification—reducing their intake as they reduce their stress through their broader plan of action. They plan to feel better and need less alcohol.

The U.S. Department of Agriculture and the U.S. Department of Health and Human Services define moderate drinking as no more than one drink a day for most women, and no more than two drinks a day for most men. Other experts define moderate drinking as two for women, three for men.

A little can even be good. Research shows that lower levels of alcohol consumption can reduce stress and promote conviviality. Moderate drinking can decrease tension, anxiety and self-consciousness. Other research shows that in the elderly, moderate drinking stimulates appetite, promotes regular bowel function and improves mood.

Lower levels of drinking also are believed to decrease the risk of death from coronary artery disease. And, of course, we all have seen articles on the heart-healthy benefits of red wine in moderation, with the French being our role models for red wine counter-balancing a diet rich with butter and sugar.

There are trade-offs, of course. Most definitely, excessive use of alcohol leads to health risks and threatens your professional and personal life.

The bottom line for the person in stress—drinking is not an activity.

Smoking

When smokers are under stress, they seek relief in a cigarette. In the short term, they may relax some. But we all know the serious long-term effects. Launching into cold-turkey smoking abstinence is probably not a good idea when you are awash in urgent stress. However, stress should not be your excuse to backslide on progress you have made in smoking reduction, or as an excuse to increase the habit.

Ask your doctor for prescription help, or try some of the over-the-counter remedies.

Sleep

Your mother was right. You need eight hours of sleep a night. Well, most of us do. If you feel there are not enough hours in a day to accomplish what must be done, you may be short-changing yourself on sleep, or be unable to sleep. Or, if you're stressed and depressed, you may be sleeping too much, as an escape. Either way, with lots of in-between, people in stress have sleep issues.

My patient "Asim" couldn't sleep, and I had to help him past the problem because he was dealing with it by jogging in the middle of the night. Even in suburban Florida, that is asking for trouble.

Asim's Toxic Stress

Asim had recently retired from a career in retail, yet, when his life should be stress-free—no more stores to run, no more angry customers, no more employee hassles—he woke up in the middle of the night in a panic. His heart raced, he was short of breath, he was full of anxiety. He was so desperate for a solution to his sleep problems that he promised me, "If you cure me, I'll give you anything you want."

Asim called it "stress," but he had panic disorder plus sleep apnea, a sleeping disorder in which a person stops breathing many times a night, sometimes for a minute or more. The sleep apnea apparently triggered the panic. When all this happened at night, his wife awoke and complained about being disturbed. So Asim did what he had done earlier in his life, manage his stress by exercise. He jogged at 3 A.M.

Once Asim understood his problems and understood that he wasn't going to die, he got well. A physician specializing in sleep apnea helped him with that, including asking Asim to keep a sleep journal. I taught him the relaxation response and got him to buy a relaxation tape. We also established a routine for him. He had to get up at a certain time and do the relaxation tape. And he could jog only in the daytime.

You must make a good night's sleep a priority in your life. Give yourself permission to go to sleep at a time that will allow seven to eight hours of sleep. Your body needs this down time to renourish after a stressful day. When you plot out your day and Do List, start by marking off your sleep time.

ASIM'S TOXIC STRESS

DIFFICULT LIFE SITUATION: Adjustment to retirement

PHYSICAL DAMAGE: Sleep apnea—gasping for breath, heart pounding, sleeplessness

DEPRESSION: Adjustment disorder with anxiety

ANXIETY: Panic disorder

ACTION PLAN: Psychotherapy to understand his problem; treatment for sleep apnea with a daily sleep schedule and self-monitoring diary; relaxation tapes for when he awoke during the night; daytime jogging only

MEDICATION: Ativan® (antianxiety), Sonata® (sleep)

BIBLIOTHERAPY: *Overcoming Insomnia: A Medical Program for Problem Sleepers* (Sweeney), *The Relaxation and Stress Reduction Workbook* (Swede and Jaffe), *The Panic Attack Recovery Book* (Swede and Jaffe)

How to Get a Good Night's Sleep

Maintain a regular bedtime and wake-up time.

Sleep in a dark, cool room.

Avoid caffeine, nicotine and alcohol in the evening.

Avoid heavy meals in the evening.

Establish a pre-bedtime ritual of winding down.

Try a hot bath an hour before bedtime.

Have a glass of milk, which contains tryptophan, a natural sleep inducer.

If you cannot sleep, get up for 20 minutes and do something boring; avoid bright light.

In the morning, turn on the lights or step out into the sunshine to "set" your biological clock.

Consider medication for short-term relief:

> Sonata®
>
> Restoril®
>
> Ambien®
>
> Melatonin (over-the-counter)
>
> Valerian root (over-the-counter)
>
> Benadryl®—50 mg of this over-the-counter drug at bedtime is helpful, too, and sometimes recommended for patients with drug or alcohol problems.

If sleep problems do not improve, you might ask your doctor to refer you to sleep lab to check for sleep apnea or other sleep disorder.

Diet for Health and Mood

Diet is a huge component in your battle against stress and for physical and mental health. My patient "Teresa" is a case in point—with an unusual motivator to change her eating habits.

Teresa's Toxic Stress

Teresa was in a major slump. She hated her job as an accountant in a large firm, and it showed. Her supervisor told her she had a bad attitude. Meantime, her boyfriend left her. Plus, Teresa was angry at herself for the weight she had gained over the last few years. It was not just a little weight. Teresa had gained 100 pounds.

It was clear that Teresa hated the weight, but I couldn't get her to make the necessary commitment to take it off. From experience, I know that a person needs motivation to accomplish what is a major change. Change is difficult. Teresa wouldn't even give up her "goodie drawer" of snacks. While the downfall of many people is nighttime snacking, Teresa snacked at work. She kept a bottom draw full of cookies and chips and other high-fat, high-calorie goodies, which she dipped into any time stress dropped in on her. She refused to give up her goodie drawer, and I said I would not work with her on her weight until she was motivated at least to do that.

Finally, we found the motivation. Sex. Teresa greatly missed her sexual relationship with her boyfriend and wanted that, if not him, back in her life. She also knew the guy with whom she wanted to have sex. Trying to get her to socialize more, I had suggested she ask this friend out for a beer after work. They hit it off—up to a point. The guy liked slender women. Teresa propositioned him. He said no. But they maintained a sense of humor about it, and they still met for beer and talked about their lives and problems and hopes.

Ultimately, the guy said, "If you lose that 100 pounds you always talk about, we'll sleep together."

Sex. That's what motivated Teresa. I had her post a picture of her sexy, more slender self on her work station, so she remembered the potential. So far, so good. She's down thirty-eight pounds and they're still friends, seeing each other regularly.

TERESA'S TOXIC STRESS

DIFFICULT LIFE SITUATION: Stressful work environment, recent break-up with boyfriend, bad attitude at work
PHYSICAL DAMAGE: Overweight, migraines, fibromyalgia, iron deficiency
DEPRESSION: Dysthymia
ANXIETY: Anxious about everything, obsessively pessimistic about outcomes
ACTION PLAN: Psychotherapy focusing on improving her self-esteem and re-structuring her negative self-statements; diet and exercise; anger management with special attention to editing out her inappropriate outbursts at work; time management; goal-setting
MEDICATION: Celexa™ (antidepressant), BuSpar® (antianxiety)
BIBLIOTHERAPY: *Sugar Busters* (Steward), *Dr. Atkins Diet Revolution* (Atkins), *The Feeling Good Handbook* (Burns), *Ten Days to Self-Esteem* (Burns)

We are an overweight society. More than sixty percent of Americans over age twenty are overweight. One quarter of American adults are clinically obese, which puts them at higher risk for heart disease, type II diabetes, high blood pressure, stroke and some cancers.

Stress eating is one culprit. Stress triggers the release of cortisol, which in turn stimulates appetite, and not just any appetite. Cortisol creates cravings for sugar and fat, the fast track to weight gain because excesses not burned by physical actions get stored for future use. Most contemporary stress does not require a physical, calorie-burning response, so you when you eat to feel better while under stress, you probably pack on pounds.

The other major stress hormone, adrenalin, signals the pancreas to crank out insulin. The result is even more hunger. Further, the carbohydrates you crave to meet the hunger raise cortisol levels, creating an evil cycle for the weight-conscious.

One study showed that sixty-six percent of super-stressed women were at risk for weight gain. With cortisol coursing through the body, cravings kick in, and so does the production of the lipoprotein lipase, an enzyme that helps the body build fat. With stress eating, the body builds fat deep in the abdomen where fat cells have four times more cortisol receptors than just below the skin. It is fat associated with the "apple shape"—people who carry their weight in the middle rather than in their hips and legs, the "pear shape." "Apples" have more heart attacks and other cardiovascular problems than "pears."

Identify Your Stress-Eating Habits

I have seen twenty-question tests to determine if you are a stress eater. Most people who turn to food in stressful times don't need a test. They know it because they do it and then they feel bad about the weight they put on, which is new stress, and the cycle perpetuates itself.

Still, I get patients who tell me they do not know why they are gaining weight or cannot lose. For them, and for most stress eaters, I recommend the Five Column Food Diary. You write down (1) WHAT you ate and calories, (2) WHEN you ate, (3) WHERE you ate, (4) WHAT YOU WERE FEELING when you ate and (5) WHAT YOU WERE THINKING.

"Eating amnesia" can undermine your diet success. You do not realize how much you ingest while cooking or while being distracted by television. Researchers found people ate fifteen percent more when eating while listening to a detective story compared with when they ate free from distractions.

People are amazed at their own behavior. They discover that they are eating because they are stressed, or because they are bored or frustrated, maybe even lonely.

I see a lot of people who eat well at breakfast and lunch but gorge on dinner, or graze through night-time TV. They are shocked at the calories they add mouthful by mouthful through the sitcoms and late-night talk shows. One study showed a shocking number of women consuming more than seventy percent of their calories after 6 P.M., when they were least likely to exercise it away. Most nutritionists advise spreading the calorie load through the day. You may sleep better, too, if you eat lighter at night.

My patient "Kenny" was a nighttime binger. Kenny, in his late thirties, lived with his elderly parents, who quarreled with him frequently because Kenny refused to get a job. Kenny's older sisters were very successful professionals, but Kenny wasn't motivated. Eventually, he will inherit enough money to never work, so he is not interested in starting any climb up a ladder. Physically, he probably couldn't climb a ladder. Kenny weighs over 350 pounds, a guy who needs two seats on the airplane.

He eats a sensible dinner with his parents, but when they go to bed, he forages. Sweets are his delight—a box of cookies, gallon of ice cream, cakes, sugary junk food all night long. He's obsessive about it and says he just cannot stop.

The source of his stress is anger and repression because his mother harasses him, his late father abused him, and he is jealous that his sisters overcame all that and were successful anyway.

I'll be honest—I never found the key to turn Kenny around. I referred him to a psychiatrist who used medication to control his mood and obsessions. Kenny is a lesson, however—get control now before your problems become too ingrained.

Research shows that self-monitoring with a food diary is one of the most effective controls for dieters. I think the food diary works so well because we don't want to write down our indulgences and mistakes, and therefore we don't stray so often. In general, however, the diary helps you to see patterns and be motivated to break away from those that cause you to overeat or overindulge in alcohol. The very best advice to yourself when you see one of those patterns—a time or place or other circumstance that causes you to overeat—is to distract yourself, eat something else, or do something else. Being aware gives you that power.

MY 5-WS FOOD DIARY

WHAT I ATE AND CALORIES	WHEN I ATE	WHERE I ATE	WHAT I WAS FEELING	WHAT I WAS THINKING

"Stop If It's Stress"

Stress eaters, all emotionally driven eaters—you need to stop before you start. Think before you eat.

It helps to know that stress-fueled craving feels exactly like hunger. The stomach muscles contract in exactly the same way. You can differentiate the two only through logic, and therefore you must stop to exercise logic. "Is it stress or is it hunger? I had dinner only two hours ago. My body shouldn't need more food so soon." Or: "I really am hungry." Another piece of logic to engage the brain is that the "feel good" response to stress-eating lasts only a few minutes, and it is usually followed by feeling bloated and guilty. Picture yourself instead as in control and however many calories slimmer. Picture the positive result of the better choice before you.

Some stress-eaters post notes to themselves on the pantry or refrigerator door: "Stop if it's stress." Each person needs to find the best "stop sign" for her own patterns of stress eating.

Stress-Eating versus "Comfort Food"

I want to differentiate between the concepts of stress eating and "comfort food." Eating a gallon of butter pecan ice cream is stress eating, or a food disorder or some other self-destructive behavior. But look what happened right after the 9/11 terrorist attacks. A wave of comfort food washed across the country. You saw it in the restaurants, the magazines and newspapers, and probably in your own home. Old-fashioned chicken pot-pie. Homemade banana pudding. Mama's meatloaf and gravy. Macaroni and cheese. The food tended to be high-fat and high-calorie, because that's how people ate in the days we were being nostalgic over—back when we barely knew the word *terrorism,* or cholesterol. You could argue that this was stress eating because we were still feeling very vulnerable. At the very least, emotions played a part in food selection.

But if you do comfort food right—you sit down with family and friends and share warm and funny memories along with your meal, and you consume reasonable portions—you really are de-stressing. Turn to comfort food on occasion, not as an escape but a celebration with family or friends.

The rest of the week, the common-sense approach is a balanced diet eaten in reasonable portions.

STOP STRESS EATING

Ask yourself, is it hunger or stress?

Post a reminder on the pantry or refrigerator door.

Post a photo of a slimmer you.

Eat 5 to 6 smaller meals rather than the big three.

Keep fruit and vegetables available for snacking.

Practice portion control.

Drink less alcohol.

Drink more water.

Cut out the caffeine.

Try a glass of water with lemon when a craving starts.

Distract yourself—detour from the refrigerator to the treadmill.

Take a walk.

Call a friend when you're tempted.

Don't stock food you've binged on before.

Know your time of greatest vulnerability and schedule an activity.

Eat only at the dining table—no TV snacks.

Use the Five-Column Food Diary.

One more matter to mention on the subject of stress and food: Almost twenty years of research at M.I.T. shows that a diet that promotes the body's production of serotonin can be helpful in stress management. Serotonin is the neurotransmitter that makes us feel calm, content and in control; it is also an appetite suppressant. Cortisol stimulates appetite; serotonin suppresses it. Antidepressants like Prozac®, Paxil® and Zoloft® stimulate the presence of serotonin. Or you can do it for yourself, to a certain degree, through diet.

The M.I.T. researchers, in *The Serotonin Solution,* explain that scientists don't know exactly what happens in the brain—does stress deplete serotonin, or does stress demand more than the brain can produce, for example. However, "all you need to know is one vital piece of information: Emotional distress affects serotonin, and for many of us this results in an overwhelming desire to eat." And, as with heightened cortisol, diminished serotonin creates cravings for carbohydrates, often in excess.

The Serotonin Solution offers diets for various kinds of lifestyles and times of eating temptation. Frankly, for most people the diets would be hard to maintain without supervision, because of the scheduling rigidity and the varying formulas for protein, starch, fruit, vegetables and fat for breakfast, lunch and dinner.

Still, I value *The Serotonin Solution* for this tip, as I interpret it. If you fuel yourself with a late afternoon snack of about 200 calories of complex carbohydrates, you may stave off the temptation to overeat in the evening. A handful of baked potato chips or pretzels sets off the chain of events in which serotonin is produced. If you are in a highly stressful work environment, you really should try this, so that the minute you get home you aren't into the Chewy Chips Ahoy. Even if you're not feeling hungry, try the 4 P.M. snack.

One surprise to the P.M.-carb-up theory is that fruit is not a good choice. Fruit is the only carbohydrate that does not stimulate serotonin, according to the MIT researchers. The P.M. snack also should be low in fat and protein.

Caffeine is another culprit in the mood and food picture. Caffeine stimulates cortisol, which leads to cravings, and is believed to reduce serotonin. Again, low levels of serotonin are associated also with food cravings, loss of sleep and depression. In her book *The Mood Cure,* Julia Ross calls stimulants like caffeine (including now-banned ephedra, diet pills, ma huang and cocaine) enemies of serotonin. Aspartame, she says, is enemy number two. Aspartame, or NutraSweet®, converts to stimulant-like substances and overpowers serotonin, she writes.

The High-Protein Diets

The Serotonin Solution diets generally are low-protein for lunch and dinner. Oddly, they are almost opposite the hottest diet regimen of the last number of years—the low-carb, high-protein diets of Dr. Atkins, Sugar Busters, Protein Power, the South Beach Diet and others. New research is validating claims that high-protein diets are highly effective and not harmful to your health. The latest study found that after six months people on the Atkins diet had lost thirty-one pounds, compared to twenty pounds for people on the American Heart Association diet, and more people had stuck with the Atkins program. This study was done at the prestigious Duke University Diet and Fitness Center by Dr. Eric Westman, an internist. He presented the findings at the annual scientific meeting of the American Heart Association. The AHA diet is a low-fat diet.

In the Duke study total cholesterol fell slightly for both groups of dieters. But those on the Atkins plan had an eleven percent increase in HDL, the good cholesterol, and a forty-nine percent decrease in triglycerides. On the AHA diet, HDL showed no change, and triglycerides fell twenty-two percent.

Opposition to the low-carb way remains, however, from establishment sources such as the American Dietetic Association and the federal government.

It is my observation that the high-protein diets are especially popular with men, including many of the doctors around the lunch table at the hospital where I am on staff. My guess is that they like meat, and they do not have an interest in learning about more complicated formulas that require calorie or fat gram counting. To be fair, I also know a woman physician who recommends the high-pro, low-carb diets to her patients. My doctor friends also tend to eat leaner cuts of meat—less saturated fat than the Dr. Atkins' version of high-protein—and that makes sense to me. A small filet and a salad are great if you can afford it.

Just be aware, while carbohydrates stimulate serotonin, high-protein foods elevate levels of dopamine and norepinephrine, both associated with anxiety and stress. Also, a long-term diet that avoids carbohydrates and therefore diminishes serotonin levels might leave you feeling a little depressed. This is one of those situations where you have to weigh the pros and cons. For most people, getting rid of the weight is a mood booster in itself.

Dr. Gott's "No-no" Diet

One of the most common sense, easy-to-understand diets I know is from newspaper columnist Dr. Peter Gott. He says "no flour, no sugar." That's it. A reader once asked if he would considered writing a book about the diet, and he replied that there was nothing more to say after "no flour, no sugar." Overeaters Anonymous also advocates the no flour, no sugar diet, adding the further requirement that all food is to be weighed and measured—a version of a food diary.

For the person who needs to lose weight and rein in stress at the same time, do what works for you, as long as it is not extreme. But observe the effects not just on your body but on your mood.

I am not a dietitian. I simply recommend that you honor your mind and body with a commitment to make better food choices. It's really a way of changing your thinking about food, and that, of course, can be difficult.

The Boy Scouts' "Be Prepared" motto works well for assuring yourself a healthy and calorie-controlled diet. People living with stress need an eating plan that is easy to understand, prepare and eat. The last thing you need is more pressure to conform to a complex diet or to prepare complicated recipes or to make food choices when you are in a rush.

Give yourself a break by planning your meals in advance. Glorify leftovers—cook once in quantity, reheat and that is one less day to cook from scratch. I know a lot of double-career couples or families who cook on Sunday and prepare a second-day quantity or other dish for Monday, maybe even Tuesday. Make Wednesday your Salad Night and let each member of the family build his own salad from the buffet of nutritious food you lay out. Do Soup and Sandwich Night for another no-stress preparation. Once those days are set, the stress of deciding is gone, the temptation to dine out (and pay more) is gone, the stress of complex preparation is gone, even clean-up is minimal.

Too many of us consume most of our daily calories after 6 P.M. Nutritionists advise that you consume only forty to fifty percent of total daily calories at dinner. There is considerable evidence that calories consumed at dinner and later are more likely to be stored as fat instead of burned off with activity.

Lunch time is difficult for many people, too, whether you are at home facing a full refrigerator of choices or at work, needing nutrition in a thirty-minute window of time. Again, planning takes the stress out. The brown bag lunch from home almost always beats the fast-food takeout bag, nutritionally and calorie-wise. Take advantage of the microwave in the office kitchen, using leftovers from home or lower-calorie prepared entrees from the freezer. If you're home for lunch, be sure to stock up on fruits and vegetables that can be eaten raw.

We often say that stress reduction is a health issue not just a time management issue. But for your health, you really do need to plan ahead for a nutritious and calorie-controlled diet.

COMMON SENSE FOR A HEALTHY DIET

DO plan ahead for lunches and dinners.

DO establish weekly "theme" nights with low-preparation foods.

DO keep the cupboard stocked with fiber-rich cereals for breakfast.

DO keep the refrigerator stocked with fresh fruit and vegetables.

DO eat three to five times a day.

DO eat a well-balanced breakfast—protein, fiber, dairy, fruit.

DO choose foods rich in omega 3 fatty acids (salmon, tuna, flaxseed, pumpkin seeds, walnuts).

DO eat protein at every meal.

DO reduce saturated fat—grill, broil or bake instead of fry.

DO eat dairy products and take calcium supplements if you are a woman.

DO take a multi-vitamin.

DO exercise portion control (read more below).

DON'T skip entire meals.

DON'T throw yourself into seriously deprivational diet mode.

DON'T set unrealistic goals for your weight or physique.

DON'T eat in front of the TV.

DON'T stock the foods you know you will overeat.

Chocolate Reward

Diet discipline does not mean total denial of foods you love. Friends and colleagues of mine from my years at Penn State, Michael and Katherine Mahoney, wrote the book *Permanent Weight Control* back in 1976. As much as I appreciate the body of research behind that book, there is one tidbit from that book and the author's own food choices that I often share with my patients. Katherine loves chocolate, but she knows she would overindulge if she gave herself the opportunity. Instead, she is prepared to make a better choice. She stocks the freezer with chocolate "kisses." When she gets a craving, she takes a single chocolate kiss from the freezer. It is ice-hard, and it takes a while to eat—but she satisfies the craving with relatively few calories. Interestingly, chocolate contains a very small amount of serotonin.

Exercise Portion Control

Portion control is another important concept for common-sense calorie-control. The fast-food industry wants us to "super-size" our orders, and that is super-sizing our bodies. Many people have lost track of what constitutes a reasonable portion or serving. Study up.

PORTION CONTROL TIPS

Size it up
- 1 serving (3 ounces) of meat is the size of a deck of cards.
- 1 serving (1 cup) of potatoes, rice or pasta looks like a tennis ball.
- 1 serving of fish is the size of your checkbook.
- 1 serving of cheese is the size of a pair of dice.
- 1 serving (2 tablespoons) of butter, peanut butter or cream cheese is the size of your thumb.

NEVER "super-size" fast food.

Eat half your restaurant fare and ask for a "doggie bag."

Ask for salad dressing on the side and dip your fork not your food.

Read the labels and know how much and how many calories are in a "serving."

Serve plates with appropriate amounts; don't serve "family style."

Use smaller plates.

Never eat out of a leftovers carton or carryout carton.

Buy individual-sized bags of pretzels or other snacks.

If you order dessert at a restaurant, share it.

Don't eat with the TV on—pay attention to what you're eating.

Don't graze while you cook.

Never eat standing up.

Okinawan Portion Control

The people of Okinawa, Japan, practice *hara hachi bu*—they stop eating when they judge that they are eighty percent "full." I've read that *hara hachi bu* is a shorthand translation of "With your stomach at eight-tenths, you won't need a doctor."

Okinawans live longer and healthier than Americans. Cheeseburgers and fries are not on their menu, of course. Their diet is high in vegetables, unrefined complex carbohydrates and soy.

Even if you do not switch to miso soup with tofu, though, you might try their *hara hachi bu.* Interestingly, it's more a brain thing than a diet thing. It takes twenty minutes for your stomach to signal your brain that it is full. If you are not paying attention to the volume you are eating, you can eat past the level at which you are really full. You can learn to determine the eighty percent full feeling only through practice. Stop when you think you might be at eighty, wait twenty minutes and see if you were right. You might take a twenty-minute walk just to keep yourself away from the temptation to eat on.

Hara hachi bu is a little different, but the price is right! Give it a try.

The Diabetes Epidemic

The American Diabetes Association defines diabetes as a disease in which the body does not produce or properly use insulin. Insulin is a hormone needed to convert sugar, starches and other food into energy for daily life. The cause of diabetes, according to the Association, continues to be a mystery, although both genetics and environmental factors such as obesity and lack of exercise appear to play roles.

The Association estimates that 17 million people in the United States, or 6.2 percent of the population, have diabetes—about a third of them undiagnosed or treated.

Diabetes increases the risk of stroke, heart attack and retinopathy that can lead to blindness. It is a serious disease and its threat should be a major incentive for all of us to get control of our weight through diet and exercise.

The Other Kind of Stress Eating—Not Eating

Karen's Toxic Stress

"Karen" is a fifteen-year-old girl who battles anorexia, the eating disorder that drives her to be unhealthily thin. She thinks of herself as fat and unattractive.

While her parents were vacationing, she stayed home, and, without their supervision, lost four pounds, down to just ninety pounds.

Her parents returned and were very angry at Karen, because she had promised to adhere to the weight-maintenance regimen they had laid out for her. They brought her to me. They were right to realize that the cure for Karen's anorexia would be based in psychology.

Their love notwithstanding, her parents were Karen's primary source of stress. Other teenagers might have coped with that pressure, but when Karen's parents pushed her, she tensed up. Her stomach became so tense that she could not eat. And a circle of dysfunction began—pressure led to not eating, which led to more criticism and less eating, and Karen lost weight.

Karen has anorexia, a specific eating disorder we think of first as a relentless pursuit of thinness. Depression is often a symptom, too, as is an overdependence or engagement with parents or family. Like the stress-eating that leads to overeating, anorexia is an emotionally driven eating behavior.

For Karen's treatment plan, we negotiated a contract by which she would add food to her diet and be rewarded for following through. We took baby steps. Karen added a protein bar in the morning and a half sandwich at lunch. If she ate more, she could take a walk in the evening, or a bike ride. She could plan ahead for a weekend outing with her friends that would take her out from her parents' eyes—providing she stuck to the contract.

The contract she made with me was a good beginning. She needed structure in her eating practices, and that is the case with a lot of people living in stress, though more often on the other end of the thin-fat spectrum. Structure and planning ahead narrow the choices to the healthiest ones. Rewards keep you motivated.

A great reward to me is that Karen now plans a career as a psychologist, to give to others what she gained from therapy.

If anorexia is a problem for you, it is critical that you get immediate medical and psychological help. For the rest of us, Karen is a reminder of how the mind and body work together.

KAREN'S TOXIC STRESS

DIFFICULT LIFE SITUATION: School pressure, family discord
PHYSICAL DAMAGE: Anorexia and bulimia
DEPRESSION: Dysthymia
ANXIETY: Social anxiety—had difficulty interacting with others at school, compulsive and very anxious about pleasing teachers and achieving good grades; perfectionist
ACTION PLAN: Psychotherapy; behavioral contracting to set goals to add food intake, set rewards for weight gain/maintenance; exercise; time-management techniques; social skills training
MEDICATION: Prozac® (antidepressant)

Summary

Your mental and physical health is dramatically affected by what you eat and how much you exercise. Food can affect your mood. Your weight and physical condition can affect your self-esteem. Exercise beats back stress. When you see how all these factors interrelate, you will do a better job of caring for yourself through diet, exercise and sleep.

Strategies and Techniques

Check-select those that will become part of your Action Plan to Recovery.

❏ Keep a 5-Column Food Diary

Plan meals ahead
       ❏ Cook ahead on the weekend
       ❏ Establish theme nights or low-preparation nights
          My theme nights are ——————————————————
       ❏ Brown-bag my lunch at work   How often? ——————————

Choose a diet for weight loss or general health
- ❏ High-protein, low carbohydrate
- ❏ Portion control or *hara hachi bu*
- ❏ Dr. Gott's "no flour, no sugar" diet
- ❏ *The Serotonin Solution* diet or afternoon snack tip
- ❏ Any reasonable diet/program that has been effective in the past

Commit to an exercise program
- ❏ Cardiovascular training (walking, running, swimming, cycling, etc.) _____ times per week
- ❏ Resistance training (weights) _____ times per week
- ❏ Flexibility training (stretching, yoga) _____ times per week
- ❏ Reduce drinking and/or smoking My goal is _____

Resolve sleep issues
- ❏ A good night's sleep a priority in my schedule
- ❏ Keep a sleep journal
- ❏ Bibliotherapy _____

Step 7

Take Charge and Create Order

When we are organized, our homes, offices and schedules reflect and encourage who we are, what we want and where we are going.
—Julie Morgenstern, *Organizing from the Inside Out*

Step 7

Take Charge and Create Order

Rene's Toxic Stress

"Rene" is a social worker who counsels drug abusers and alcoholics. These are very difficult people with problems that are not easily mitigated.

She came to me because she had "hit the wall." In my practice I see many businesspeople who tell me they have "hit rock bottom" or are "burned out." These are successful people in professional environments that value productivity and, like Rene, are self-motivated high-achievers with a passion for their work.

Rene was more than burned-out, however. A coworker had died, and another coworker was home recuperating from surgery, leaving Rene with a triple workload. Sometimes she saw fifty clients a day. She did her best, but she began having anxiety and panic attacks while driving to work. After a day of dealing with a difficult clientele, she would come home and be overcome with feelings of fatigue, helplessness and hopelessness. She was occasionally delusional, and all this drove her to thoughts of suicide.

Rene knew she had to get help, and she did.

RENE'S TOXIC STRESS

DIFFICULT LIFE SITUATION: Overload at work, a difficult clientele and unsympathetic supervisors; nothing in her life but work

PHYSICAL DAMAGE: She was working with a neurologist for a ringing in her ears; she was not sleeping at all

DEPRESSION: Major depressive episode

ANXIETY: Severe, with panic disorder

ACTION PLAN: Psychotherapy; cognitive restructuring; referral to a psychiatrist for medications; a medical leave of absence from work; problem-solving to reconsider her career choice

MEDICATION: Seroquel™ (antipsychotic), Effexor® (antidepressant), Klonopin® (antianxiety), Ambien® (sleep)

BIBLIOTHERAPY: *Peace from Nervous Suffering* (Weekes), *A Guide to Rational Living* (Ellis), *Women and Anxiety* (DeRosis), *Feeling Good: The New Mood Therapy* (Burns)

For Rene, the start of her solution was a medical leave of absence. She didn't want to do it, but her neurologist and I agreed this was best. When her physical health improves, we will problem-solve for the future.

Take Control by Creating Balance in Your Life

We all need balance, and one way I work with people who are in burnout is an exercise I call Pie Chart of My Life. Businesspeople are accustomed to pie charts and similar analysis, so it works well.

They draw a circle, and I ask them to draw the portion of their waking lives that is "work." I ask them to fill in a slice for family, then leisure pleasure, exercise and spiritual connection. As you can imagine, the work slice usually dominates. For Rene, work was the entire circle. She had nothing else.

Next, I ask patients to draw a Pie Chart of My Life as they would like it to be. Executives in burn-out often experience depression and generally have a hard time allowing themselves adequate time for pleasure. I tell them they need to create more time for the things they enjoy. They need to rejuvenate. They need a change of pace and scenery. Travel. Exercise. Pleasant activities.

Please do the Pie Chart of My Life Exercise before proceeding in this chapter.

Pie Chart of My Life as It is
Draw in slices of the circle for

W – Work
F – Family
LP – Leisure pleasure
E – Exercise/recreational activity
S – Spiritual connection

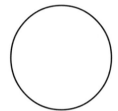

Pie Chart of My Life as I Would Like It
Draw in slices of the circle for

W – Work
F – Family
LP – Leisure pleasure
E – Exercise/recreational activity
S – Spiritual connection

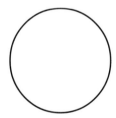

Please keep this notion of the right balance in mind as you proceed with this chapter.

The Work Component

Frank's Toxic Stress

"Frank" is a former VP of a Fortune 500 company. Only a few years ago he was running factories in the United States and internationally, responsible for thousands of employees and millions in revenue. Frank's core identity was that of a powerful executive. When he retired, he lost that identity. He said doing nothing was more stressful than running a corporate division. When his wife died, he sank into depression because he did not have the driving demand that kept him motivated and self-fulfilled.

For many people the work component is way out of balance. It's the American way—achieve, compete, get ahead. I encourage you to give serious consideration to whether your work component takes away too much time from family and health. I know a great many physicians who are sacrificing too much in order to repay college loans, establish big practices, avoid malpractice lawsuits or make a name for themselves. Job burnout is preventable, but it takes foresight and acceptance of where the lines must be drawn to be professionally successfully while having a meaningful private life, as well.

FRANK'S TOXIC STRESS

DIFFICULT LIFE SITUATION: Retirement, death of his wife
PHYSICAL DAMAGE: Sleep apnea, heart-lung complications
DEPRESSION: Major depressive episode
ANXIETY: Anxious over how to find a fulfilling life in retirement
ACTION PLAN: Treatment for sleep apnea; problem-solving to find volunteer roles and teaching assignments in which he could share his executive expertise
MEDICATION: Zoloft® (antidepressant), Sonata® (sleep)

Basic Time, Place and Organizational Management

Recovery from toxic stress is a whole-life change, addressing many different aspects of your thinking, behavior and habits. Stress management, focusing primarily on relieving symptoms, is *not* sufficient to rid your life of toxic stress. Stress management, time management and organizational structuring, however, are very beneficial. When you remove some of the "little things," you can work on the "bigger" things, like the depression and anxiety. The little things can mount up and become a major obstacle, and therefore whittling them down to size is extremely valuable to you.

Here are the best tips I know on time, place and organizational management, gathered from colleagues, the Franklin Planner system, books, patients and friends over many years. Patty's friend Phyliss Reily in California also contributed. Patty says Phyliss is the Queen of Organization. When she asked her for tips, Phyliss wrote back and said she had been keeping notes on her organization practices and as soon as she organized them, she would send them! As you read through, mark the ones with which you know you have trouble.

Anti-Stress Time Management
Check those that may need attention.

❑ Learn how to say no—there is a limit to how much I can do and maintain health.

❑ Do less—I don't have to be perfect or "have it all."

❑ Don't over commit myself or family.

❑ Keep my TO DO TODAY list short.

❑ Divide my TO DO lists into WORK and PERSONAL sections.

❑ Revise my work-related tomorrow's TO DO TODAY list before leaving the office, so I can leave work at work and move on to my personal life.

❑ Plan the order in which I will do things and estimate time frames.

❑ Keep my TO DO SOONISH list current but give myself time to get to it.

❑ Do the tasks I like least first—reduce the procrastination factor, or do the hardest tasks first.

❑ Keep a daily, weekly and monthly planner in whatever format works best for me—a personal planner with loose-leaf pages and sections for telephone numbers and other information, or a personal digital assistant that is compatible with my computer.

❑ Every day plan my appointments, things to do, phone calls, errands, etc.

❑ Make daily goals.
Prioritize them into A, B, and C. A is the absolute priority item that has to be completed that day. B is moderately important but can be done over the next couple of days. C is not of immediate importance, but I will slowly work at it and in a couple of days it may move to the A category.

❑ Set goals for the week and the specific strategies I will use to accomplish them.

❑ Set longer-term goals, projects to accomplish in the near future, with timelines.

❑ Shop efficiently.

   ❑ Shop for groceries no more than twice a week.

   ❑ Organize my shopping list by category, or better, by aisles of my regular store (many stores provide a guide at the checkout counter).

   ❑ Create a master list of my grocery shopping based on items I routinely buy, print extra copies, then just check what I need instead of starting from scratch each week—a good reminder system.

   ❑ Bulk-shop at discount stores if I have storage space—stock up on laundry products, paper towels, toilet tissues, bath and dish soap; aim for enough supplies for four months.

   ❑ One-stop shop: Frequent grocery stores that feature delis, bakeries, banks, photo development, Western Union, pharmacy, dry cleaners, and sell postage stamps. Reduce my time in the car.

❑ Maintain a daily calendar for all family members; consider color-coding for each member of the family (keep colored pens handy).

❑ Schedule exercise, relaxation, pleasurable activities.

❑ Delegate, delegate, delegate.

❑ Check back with people to whom I delegate.

❑ Manage my e-mail: Answer promptly, but don't feel obligated to respond in detail if I don't have the time.

❑ Ask for help.

❑ Clear my desk at the end of the day.

❑ Run a tight meeting—start on time, end on time.

❑ Prepare for the office the night before: cell phone in charger; keys, purse, briefcase ready to go.

❑ Prepare the family each evening for the day ahead; know what I will wear and make for the children's and/or my lunches.

❑ Cluster my phone time.

❑ Cluster my errands.

❑ Schedule family time.
❑ Reward myself.
❑ Be courteous but efficient in telephone conversations.
❑ Turn the TV off and the music on.
❑ Use sticky notes for reminders.

Myra's Toxic Stress

"Myra" found herself in a position that is more and more familiar in contemporary society. She tried to be "Super Mom" and burned out amid the chaos of a blended family. It was the second marriage for both of them. He had two children by his first wife, and because Myra so wanted children, they had two children together. Now, his oldest at age twenty returned to the home, bringing with her an out-of-wedlock infant.

Myra worked at home writing newsletters for chiropractors and others in the medical community. It was a full-time job with deadline pressure and clients to please. But she and her husband also lived a life along fairly traditional marriage roles—she was the cook, chauffeur, housecleaner, child-rearer, in addition to her job. She felt a huge responsibility to do it all and do it very well.

Myra came to me when depression and panic attacks put her over the edge. She had great sadness, no energy, and frequently cried. She swallowed her anger, and the build-up produced panic attacks. In perimenopause, she had some hormonal peaks and valleys affecting her mood, as well as a thyroid that was acting up.

Through psychotherapy, we came to understand that Myra was angry at her husband for some long-ago choices, as well as for letting the grown daughter take advantage of Myra. With little notice or appreciation, the daughter often left the baby at home for Myra to care for while the daughter went out with friends. She had missed out on the fun part of being a teenager because of the baby and was trying to make up for lost time. She helped out at home very little.

In the problem-solving phase of our work together Myra realized the importance of creating more order in her home life and in giving herself some time off from the fray. In her Action Plan, she pledged to:

- be more assertive in getting family members to help out—delegate more;
- let go of some of her anger;
- "contract" with the grown daughter—Myra would babysit on Friday nights if the daughter would make dinner for the family on Saturday nights;
- do something pleasurable for herself every day.

Myra and her husband both made out a version of the Pleasure File in which they recorded 10 Things To Do for Myself. This amounted to giving themselves permission to detach from the chaos. Myra had never had a manicure, and that was one of her entries. Myra and her husband said this one thing, the Pleasure File, was the best thing they ever did for their happiness.

Creating order is not just moving things around the house or getting a new PDA. Creating order often is about working with other people in your family or environment to take the pressure off you. It can be about changing expectations, too.

MYRA'S TOXIC STRESS

DIFFICULT LIFE SITUATION: Chaotic home life of a blended family; unresolved anger; overworked and unappreciated homemaker

PHYSICAL DAMAGE: Perimenopausal hormone swings, thyroid problem

DEPRESSION: Major depressive episode, recurrent

ANXIETY: Panic attacks fueled by anger

ACTION PLAN: Psychotherapy; journaling to deal with long-ago choice about abortion and jealousy over her husband's indulgence of children; self-esteem workbook and assertiveness training; use of Pleasure File

MEDICATION: Effexor® (antidepressant)

BIBLIOTHERAPY: *Ten Days to Self-Esteem!* (Burns), *Feeling Good* (Burns), *When I Say No, I Feel Guilty* (Smith)

Clutter and Disorder Take a Toll

In our pursuit of health, wealth and happiness, Americans in general amass a lot of stuff. There may be some people who live stressless in a cluttered environment, but most of us are calmer when there is order and we know where to find things when we need them. Therefore, a piece of stress management is clutter management. Simplify, simplify, simplify.

Here, again, is common sense advice on simplifying and organizing your home environment. Your home should be your Safe Zone. I sometimes tell people to envision a castle surrounded by a moat, and at night, pull up the drawbridge so the pressures of the work day cannot come in. Serenity in your surroundings is one of those Martha Stewart "good things." Begin with Ben Franklin's philosophy: "A place for everything, and everything in its place."

How to Simplify "Stuff" at Home
(Check those that need attention.)

❑ Organize personal files for easy access
    ❑ Keep warranties and guarantees file by categories: large and small appliances, computer hardware, computer software, TV-VCR-DVD, miscellaneous.
    ❑ Keep an Important Records file (birth certificates, passports, divorce decrees).
    ❑ Keep a "ticket drawer," so I'll always know where the concert or game tickets are.
    ❑ Maintain all medical records.
    ❑ Keep auto maintenance records in the glove compartment.
    ❑ Maintain a family information directory with names of doctors, teachers, repair people, etc.; keeping plastic insert pages of business cards is helpful at home as well as at work; a Rolodex works well too.
❑ Twice a year clean the closets.
❑ Keep an emergency kit in the car and be prepared for natural disasters.
❑ Keep a toiletry/overnight bag ready for a last-minute trip.
❑ Use bleach hand-wipes for quick bathroom cleanup.
❑ Keep a squeegee in the shower and after each shower use spray that eliminates soap buildup.
❑ Before Christmas, have children give their old toys to charity.
❑ Keep toys in clear plastic bins with lids.

❑ Toys that aren't put away go into the Penalty Box for a day.
❑ Keep the gas tank at least one-quarter full—for emergencies and anti-stress insurance.
❑ Add shelves in closets.
❑ Clean the refrigerator before grocery shopping.
❑ Schedule and assign home chores.
❑ Clear the floors and tabletops before going to bed (and share this duty).
❑ Store rarely used kitchen appliances under counters.
❑ Toss old magazines once a month.
❑ Toss newspapers daily.
❑ Sort the mail immediately and discard the junk.
❑ Empty the dishwasher every night.
❑ Make the bed every morning and require everyone else in the family to do so too.

Laundry

    ❑ Sort dirty clothes into hampers for whites, colors, dry-cleaners.
    ❑ Collect and distribute clothes by color-coded hampers for various family members.
    ❑ Schedule laundry duty (Monday mornings? one load every morning before work? Sunday night?).
    ❑ Buy no-iron clothing.
    ❑ Maintain extra laundry supplies.

❑ Keep shoes on racks or shelves in the closet.
❑ Give away/toss old linens, towels.
❑ Have a garage sale once a year.
❑ Throw away old garden tools that are not used.
❑ Give away the appliances and power tools that are not used.
❑ Bring in fresh flowers.

Money and Stress

Who hasn't felt stress over money? Whether it's making ends meet or bankruptcy or conflicting values about money in a marriage or how to save for your children's college and your retirement as well—money breeds stress and anxiety. If money is high on your stress scale, I strongly advise getting some financial advice. Start with your own bank or a financial planner recommended by your bank or a trusted friend. But remember that in the end, you are the one who will solve your issues, because you have the power to choose.

I am sharing the universal basics of money management in the accompanying box. Almost all of us can benefit from a review of these.

ANTI-STRESS MONEY MANAGEMENT

Check those that need improvement.

❑ Live within my means.
❑ Create a family budget and live by it.
❑ Make a plan for paying off debt.
❑ Build an emergency "cushion" in the bank.
❑ Make one morning or night a week an "office time" for paying personal bills, keeping track of records, making appointments.
❑ Consolidate services, such as cell and home phone billing.
❑ Consolidate stocks holdings to one investment firm or advisor.
❑ Pay some bills by automatic deduction from my checking account.
❑ Pay bills on-line.
❑ Balance my checkbook.
❑ Educate myself about savings and investments.
❑ Insure myself to protect the family.
❑ Invest in a home or condo.
❑ Keep a tax deductions file.
❑ Use only one credit card; pay it off monthly.
❑ Save, save, save.
  ❑ Pay myself first with savings.
  ❑ Look ahead to retirement and know what I will need.
  ❑ Invest for the children's education.
  ❑ Take full advantage of 401k matching programs.
  ❑ Pay into an IRA annually.
❑ Get investment and estate planning advice I can trust.

Summary

Time, place and organizational management can diminish the chaos and confusion in your life. Sometimes even just one small change can make a big difference in your life. This is self-discipline, but it is also consistency. Consistency and predictability prevent stress. You carefully record entries on your calendars. You prioritize and do not overcommit to projects or events. If there's a "ticket drawer," you never have to experience the anxiety of foraging for them amid the stacks of paper on your desktop. People with toxic stress cannot always eliminate the major source of their stress—being a caregiver or living with an alcoholic—but there are some time, place and organizational management remedies that can diminish the lesser stressors. And it is worth the effort, because stress is cumulative, and the more you have, the worse the attack on your immune system.

In this step you self-diagnosed areas in which you need improvement in time management, home and work organization and personal finance. The Pie Chart of My Life provided perspective on balance in your life.

Strategies and Techniques

List the resolutions that will become part of your Action Plan to Recovery.

❑ Practice time management at work

_____

_____

_____

❑ Practice time management at home

_____

_____

_____

❑ Organize my environment

_____

_____

_____

❑ Practice money management

_____

_____

_____

❑ Bibliotherapy

_____

_____

_____

Your 7-Steps-to-Recovery Action Plan

Your 7-Steps-to-Recovery Action Plan

Recovery from toxic stress requires some soul-searching and commitment. You are the critical player. You have to want to change, you have to make the changes. Gail Sheehy has written insightfully about life stages and how we sometimes get stuck in the rocky transitions between them. It is true for many of the patients you have read about in this book.

It is also true that those patients overcame their toxic stress, or lessened it to a more tolerable level. You can achieve that success, too. Your commitment to change is the real key. No book, no therapist, no wishful thinking can do it for you. It is imperative, therefore, that you persuade yourself of the value, and I have found a technique often used in counseling people with alcohol or drug abuse to be helpful to all persons needing that self-persuasion to change habits and lifestyle—in your case, to commit to an Action Plan for Recovery from toxic stress and attempt to make the changes that will de-stress your life.

You can begin to look at a change process with a technique called "Decisional Balancing." This method asks you to (a) think about the benefits and costs of your current choices (and let's use the alcohol abuse as the example) and (b) think about what it would take to change your choices.

In business and in many other areas of your life, you weigh the pros and cons, or the benefits and costs—to add a product line, or not; to put inventory on sale, or not; to hire more staff, or not. You base your decisions on whether the advantages outweigh the disadvantages. You may have made your choice to over-use alcohol, in our example, because you thought the pleasure to yourself outweighed any damage to yourself or others. On the other hand, you may never have analyzed your situation so carefully.

You can use this chart to analyze the benefits of changing your life (or alcohol abuse or of continuing in an abusive relationship, or letting your anger get the best of you, or any of the other behaviors and choices contributing to your toxic stress). Fill in the squares with your assessment of the benefits and costs of changing, and the benefits and costs of not changing. Think about what you stand to lose and gain, how your situation affects your health, your relationships, your work, your overall happiness.

Here are examples from a Decisional Balancing exercise on overuse of alcohol:

CHANGING	NOT CHANGING
BENEFITS OF Increased control over my life Improved health and illness prevention Happier home life Renewed respect of family, friends, co-workers Renewed job security	BENEFITS OF Enjoy socializing over drinks It's relaxing at end of day Eases inhibitions
COSTS OF Loss of pleasurable activity Embarrassment Boredom Loss of stress reliever	COSTS OF Disapproval by family, friends Loss of respect, and self-respect Risk losing friends, family Risk job security, advancement Likely health damage Drunk driving potential Financial cost

At the end of this exercise, think about whether the costs of your situation outweigh the benefits of continuing your behaviors or circumstances. Changing versus not changing. I can tell you right now, if you have toxic stress, change wins. You just have to see it in your own terms.

You may want to use Decisional Balancing to help you analyze your overall toxic stress, or core components such as depression, anxiety, or for specific behaviors, such as alcohol abuse.

After reading the 7 Steps, I hope you have not only gotten relief from some of the physical torments of your toxic stress but also that you have gained insight into the core problems in your life. To keep you on track to recovery, I strongly recommend that you make your commitment in writing on the 7-Step Action Plan worksheet in this concluding chapter of the book. If you can, photocopy it and pass it along to a friend, or keep a fresh copy for yourself so you can revise it as you progress. I advise all my patients, "Ink it, don't think it" because writing down your self-promises and your goals fosters commitment.

For each step, you will set goals. I teach an entire seminar on goal-setting, but here is the quick version:

- Set realistic short-term and long-term goals that directly address your symptoms and the sources of your stress. Do not over commit and set yourself up for failure.
- Make those goals measurable—frequency, time expended, dollars spent.
- Prioritize the top three and dedicate the most time and energy to those.
- Using imagery and visualization, consider the impact your accomplishments will have on your life.
- Review your Action Plan at the beginning of each month, evaluating your performance as well as the effectiveness of the strategies and techniques. Revise and re-prioritize as you see need.
- Reward yourself for your achievements.

When you create an Action Plan, the best predictor of its success is the self-reward plan that is connected to each entry. Connect a reward to each task or goal completed and be sure to follow through with rewards to yourself. You will feel good about your accomplishments and feel justified in the well-earned rewards.

Working through the seven steps, set your goals. Tell yourself what you will do to regain control of your life, or to find balance, or resolve your conflicts. Then choose which strategies you will employ.

Change is hard. Research shows that it takes thirty days to create a new habit. You have to really want that change to stick with it for thirty days. But tell yourself, after thirty days you will "own" it, and it no longer will be so hard. It will be automatic. With toxic stress, there's usually an "aha" moment when you know you have to change, when the pain or the torment reach an intolerable level. Remember your "aha" moment whenever you slip from your commitment.

Of course, with toxic stress, we're talking many changes—across relationships, at home and work, in how you think, and in how you take care of yourself. That is why you need the personalized Action Plan—in writing. You won't be perfect in getting everything done, but that's OK. Over the long haul, there is a big payoff. You become a happier, healthier person. And that is when you know you have truly recovered from toxic stress

My 7-Step Action Plan to Recovery from Toxic Stress

Self-Diagnosis Summarized

Do I have toxic stress?   Yes ❑   No ❑   Maybe ❑

Difficult life situation (stressors)? (describe) _____

_____

Physical damage? (describe) _____

Depression? (describe) _____

_____

Anxiety? (describe) _____

_____

Yes, no or maybe, your Personal Action Plan will guide you to getting your life back under control and handling stressors more effectively.

My Goals for Recovery

Express these in "I statements."

      I want to feel

- _____
- _____

      I want to change

- _____
- _____

      My rewards will be

- _____
- _____

STEP 1. UNDERSTAND STRESS AND THE MIND-BODY CONNECTION

Things to think about: Self-diagnosis will help you understand how stress is attacking your body, and how you must find ways to turn off the stress hormones at least periodically to let your body rest and restore. Journaling can help you clarify the sources of your stress, the physical symptoms that may be related, and the feelings you have for your situation and yourself.

Strategies and Techniques

(select and commit to frequency)

❏ Journaling   Where? _____   How often? _____

❏ Bibliotherapy _____

STEP 2. DIG OUT OF DEPRESSION

Things to think about: About one in six Americans will experience depression in their lifetimes, so acknowledging your own condition should not frighten you. It is very treatable, and the techniques used in psychotherapy are well documented as successful.

Strategies and Techniques

(select and commit to frequency)

Seek professional help
- ❏ Talk to a doctor
- ❏ Make an appointment
- ❏ Consider medications (prescription or herbal)

❏ Assess yourself with the Beck Depression Inventory or other depression screening tests.   How often _____

❏ Bibliotherapy _____

Recognize distorted thinking
- ❏ Use cognitive restructuring   When? _____
- ❏ Use the Triple-Column Technique to repair distorted thinking
  When?   _____

❏ Create a Pleasure File   Use when?   _____
❏ Try art, music or dance therapy   How often?   _____
❏ Try light therapy   How often?   _____
❏ Pet therapy
❏ Reduce alcohol consumption and eliminate illegal drug use
❏ Join a support group

Step 3. Defeat Anxiety and Anger

Things to think about: Anxiety, anger and stress elicit the same harmful hormones that wreak the same damaging physical effects. There are many effective techniques to relieve stress symptoms and achieve relaxation. Anger management can help you as well.

Strategies and Techniques

(select and commit to frequency)
- ❏ Self-assess your anxiety
- ❏ Seek psychotherapy with a mental health professional
- ❏ Practice panic attack responses
- ❏ Use breathing techniques to relax
  - ❏ Relaxation breathing   How often? _____
  - ❏ Deep Breathing   How often? _____
  - ❏ Yoga's alternate nostril breathing   How often? _____
- ❏ Use progressive muscle relaxation   How often? _____
- ❏ Use cognitive behavioral rehearsal
- ❏ Practice assertive responses
- ❏ Create your own thought-stopping technique
- ❏ Self-diagnose anger
- ❏ Self-coach for anger management   When? _____
- ❏ Meditation   When? _____
- ❏ Prayer   When? _____
- ❏ Use relaxation techniques. Choose a therapeutic form of relaxation.
  - ❏ Massage   How often? _____
  - ❏ Aromatherapy   When? _____
  - ❏ Hydrotherapy   When? _____
- ❏ Bibliotherapy _____

STEP 4. THINK WITH THE "BRIGHT SIDE" OF YOUR BRAIN

Things to think about: Positive thinking, optimism, common sense, humor—they're all better for you than their darker partners. If you change the way you think, you can change the way you feel and behave.

Strategies and Techniques

(select and commit to frequency)

❑ Practice loving self-talk
❑ Post and use daily affirmations
❑ Practice optimism   Specific goals?   _____
❑ Post a reminder of any positive-thinking tips to be worked on
❑ Create a mental video   Situation?   _____
❑ Humorous reading, music, movies   How often?   _____
❑ Do a humor inventory
❑ Find a humor ally   Who?   _____
❑ Smile more
❑ Bibliotherapy   _____

STEP 5. LOVE AND BE LOVED

Things to think about: For couples the Big Five of Stressors in a relationship, beginning with the most common, are (1) power and control issues, (2) the children, (3) money, (4) division of responsibilities and (5) sex. Your relationship may be the source of your stress, or it may be your refuge from it. Living in toxic stress, you need a lot of love, empathy, friendship and a support system to help when times are bad. Divorce prevention is choosing the right mate from the outset.

Strategies and Techniques

(select and commit to frequency)

Make connections
        ❑ Turn to your support system   Who?   _____
        ❑ Vent to a friend or family member   Who?   _____
            When?   _____

❏ Join, join, join   What? _____

Frequency of participation? _____

Show love

    ❏ Choose from tips such as a daily niceness

    I will show love by   _____

    _____

    ❏ Arrange a Mystery Marriage Weekend   How often? _____

❏ Practice Rules of Engagement for Couples in Conflict

    When to use? _____

❏ Set aside "Couch Time"   When to use? _____

❏ Agree to use time-outs

❏ Define your "Three Wishes" for improving your life together

_____

_____

_____

❏ Commit to "Words to Stay Married By"

❏ Forgive

❏ Spell out your Psychic Restitution—What Would It Take?

_____

Improve parenting

    ❏ Use behavior modification for the children

    ❏ Use consequences not punishment   How? _____

    _____

❏ Be smart about dating.   My rules are: _____

_____

❏ Bibliotherapy _____

STEP 6. COMMIT TO HEALTH AND WELLNESS

Things to think about: Exercise is the number one de-stressor. You can plan and organize your eating habits to get control of your weight. The payoffs for getting your weight under control are huge—avoid diabetes and protect your heart.

Strategies and Techniques

(select and commit to frequency)

❑ Keep a 5-Column Food Diary

Plan meals ahead

  ❑ Cook ahead on the weekend
  ❑ Establish theme nights or low-preparation nights
    My theme nights are _____
  ❑ Brown-bag my lunch at work How often? _____

Choose a diet for weight loss or general health

  ❑ High-protein, low carbohydrate
  ❑ Portion control or *hara hachi bu*
  ❑ Dr. Gott's "no flour, no sugar" diet
  ❑ *The Serotonin Solution* diet or afternoon snack tip
  ❑ Any reasonable diet/program that has been effective in the past

Commit to an exercise program

  ❑ Cardiovascular training (walking, running, swimming, cycling, etc.)
    _____ times per week
  ❑ Resistance training (weights) _____ times per week
  ❑ Flexibility training (stretching, yoga) _____ times per week
❑ Reduce drinking and/or smoking My goal is _____

Resolve sleep issues

  ❑ A good night's sleep a priority in my schedule
  ❑ Keep a sleep journal
❑ Bibliotherapy   _____

Step 7. Take Charge and Create Order

Things to think about: Time management and organization are a matter of self-discipline. Even if you cannot control all the stressors in your life, you can eliminate some.

Strategies and Techniques
(select and commit to frequency)

❑ Create the Pie Chart of My Life as I Want It to Be

Draw in slices of the circle for
      W — Work
      F — Family
    LP — Leisure pleasure
      E — Exercise/recreational activity
      S — Spiritual connection

❑ Practice time management at work

_____

_____

❑ Practice time management at home

_____

_____

❑ Organize my environment

_____

_____

❑ Practice money management

_____

_____

❑ Bibliotherapy   _____

Appendix

Diagnostic Criteria

Reprinted with permission from the *Diagnostic and Statistical Manual of Mental Disorders,* Fourth Edition, Text Revision. Copyright 2000 American Psychiatric Association.

Mood Episodes
Major Depressive Episode

    A. Five (or more) of the following symptoms have been present during the same 2-week period and represent a change from previous functioning; at least one of the symptoms is either (1) depressed mood or (2) loss of interest or pleasure.

    Note: Do not include symptoms that are clearly due to a general medical condition, or mood-incongruent delusions or hallucinations.

    (1) depressed mood most of the day, nearly every day, as indicated by either subjective report (e.g., feels sad or empty) or observation made by others (e.g., appears tearful). Note: In children and adolescents, can be irritable mood.

    (2) markedly diminished interest or pleasure in all, or almost all, activities most of the day, nearly every day (as indicated by either subjective account or observation made by others)

    (3) significant weight loss when not dieting or weight gain (e.g., a change of more than 5% of body weight in a month), or decrease or increase in appetite nearly every day. Note: In children, consider failure to make expected weight gains.

    (4) insomnia or hypersomnia nearly every day

    (5) psychomotor agitation or retardation nearly every day (observable by others, not merely subjective feelings of restlessness or being slowed down)

(6) fatigue or loss of energy nearly every day

(7) feelings of worthlessness or excessive or inappropriate guilt (which may be delusional) nearly every day (not merely self-reproach or guilt about being sick)

(8) diminished ability to think or concentrate, or indecisiveness, nearly every day (either by subjective account or as observed by others)

(9) recurrent thoughts of death (not just fear of dying), recurrent suicidal ideation without a specific plan, or a suicide attempt or a specific plan for committing suicide

B. The symptoms do not meet criteria for a Mixed Episode.

C. The symptoms cause clinically significant distress or impairment in social, occupational, or other important areas of functioning.

D. The symptoms are not due to the direct physiological effects of a substance (e.g., a drug of abuse, a medication) or a general medical condition (e.g., hypothyroidism).

E. The symptoms are not better accounted for by Bereavement, i.e., after the loss of a loved one, the symptoms persist for longer than 2 months or are characterized by marked functional impairment, morbid preoccupation with worthlessness, suicidal ideation, psychotic symptoms, or psychomotor retardation.

Depressive Disorders

296.2x Major Depressive Disorder, Single Episode

A. Presence of a single Major Depressive Episode.

B. The Major Depressive Episode is not better accounted for by Schizoaffective Disorder and is not superimposed on Schizophrenia, Schizophreniform Disorder, Delusional Disorder, or Psychotic Disorder Not Otherwise Specified.

C. There has never been a Manic Episode, a Mixed Episode, or a Hypomanic Episode. Note: This exclusion does not apply if all of the manic-like, mixed-like, or hypomanic-like episodes are substance or treatment induced or are due to the direct physiological effects of a general medical condition.

If the full criteria are currently met for a Major Depressive Episode, *specify* its current clinical status and/or features:

Mild, Moderate, Severe Without Psychotic Features/Severe
With Psychotic Features
    Chronic
    With Catatonic Features
    With Melancholic Features
    With Atypical Features
    With Postpartum Onset

If the full criteria are not currently met for a Major Depressive Episode, *specify* the current clinical status of the Major Depressive Disorder or features of the most recent episode:
In Partial Remission, In Full Remission
    Chronic
    With Catatonic Features
    With Melancholic Features
    With Atypical Features
    With Postpartum Onset

296.3x Major Depressive Disorder, Recurrent
    A. Presence of two or more Major Depressive Episodes.
       Note: To be considered separate episodes, there must be an interval of at least 2 consecutive months in which criteria are not met for a Major Depressive Episode.
    B. The Major Depressive Episodes are not better accounted for by Schizoaffective Disorder and are not superimposed on Schizophrenia, Schizophreniform Disorder, Delusional Disorder, or Psychotic Disorder Not Otherwise Specified.
    C. There has never been a Manic Episode, a Mixed Episode, or a Hypomanic Episode. Note: This exclusion does not apply if all of the manic-like, mixed-like, or hypomanic-like episodes are substance or treatment induced or are due to the direct physiological effects of a general medical condition.

If the full criteria are currently met for a Major Depressive Episode, *specify* its current clinical status and/or features:

Mild, Moderate, Severe Without Psychotic Features/Severe
With Psychotic Features
    Chronic
    With Catatonic Features
    With Melancholic Features
    With Atypical Features
    With Postpartum Onset
       If the full criteria are not currently met for a Major Depressive Episode, *specify* the current clinical status of the Major Depressive Disorder or features of the most recent episode:
In Partial Remission, In Full Remission
    Chronic
    With Catatonic Features
    With Melancholic Features
    With Atypical Features
    With Postpartum Onset
Specify:
Longitudinal Course Specifiers (With and Without Interepisode Recovery)
With Seasonal Pattern

300.4 Dysthymic Disorder
    A. Depressed mood for most of the day, for more days than not, as indicated either by subjective account or observation by others, for at least 2 years. Note: In children and adolescents, mood can be irritable and duration must be at least 1 year.
    B. Presence, while depressed, of two (or more) of the following:
        (1) poor appetite or overeating
        (2) insomnia or hypersomnia
        (3) low energy or fatigue
        (4) low self-esteem
        (5) poor concentration or difficulty making decisions
        (6) feelings of hopelessness
    C. During the 2-year period (1 year for children or adolescents) of the disturbance, the person has never been without the symptoms in Criteria A and B for more than 2 months at a time.

D. No Major Depressive Episode has been present during the first 2 years of the disturbance (1 year for children and adolescents); i.e., the disturbance is not better accounted for by chronic Major Depressive Disorder, or Major Depressive Disorder, In Partial Remission.
Note: There may have been a previous Major Depressive Episode provided there was a full remission (no significant signs or symptoms for 2 months) before development of the Dysthymic Disorder. In addition, after the initial 2 years (1 year in children or adolescents) of Dysthymic Disorder, there may be superimposed episodes of Major Depressive Disorder, in which case both diagnoses may be given when the criteria are met for a Major Depressive Episode.

E. There has never been a Manic Episode, a Mixed Episode, or a Hypomanic Episode, and criteria have never been met for Cyclothymic Disorder.

F. The disturbance does not occur exclusively during the course of a chronic Psychotic Disorder, such as Schizophrenia or Delusional Disorder.

G. The symptoms are not due to the direct physiological effects of a substance (e.g., a drug of abuse, a medication) or a general medical condition (e.g., hypothyroidism).

H. The symptoms cause clinically significant distress or impairment in social, occupational, or other important areas of functioning.

Specify if:
Early Onset: if onset is before age 21 years
Late Onset: if onset is at age 21 years or older
Specify (for most recent 2 years of Dysthymic Disorder):
With Atypical Features

311 Depressive Disorder Not Otherwise Specified
The Depressive Disorder Not Otherwise Specified category includes disorders with depressive features that do not meet the criteria for Major Depressive Disorder, Dysthymic Disorder, Adjustment Disorder With Depressed Mood, or Adjustment Disorder With Mixed Anxiety and Depressed Mood. Sometimes depressive symptoms can present as part of an Anxiety Disorder Not Otherwise Specified. Examples of Depressive Disorder Not Otherwise Specified include

1. Premenstrual dysphoric disorder: in most menstrual cycles during the past year, symptoms (e.g., markedly depressed mood, marked anxiety, marked affective lability, decreased interest in activities) regularly occurred during the last week of the luteal phase (and remitted within a few days of the onset of menses). These symptoms must be severe enough to markedly interfere with work, school, or usual activities and be entirely absent for at least 1 week postmenses (see Appendix B in DSM-IV-TR for suggested research criteria).

2. Minor depressive disorder: episodes of at least 2 weeks of depressive symptoms but with fewer than the five items required for Major Depressive Disorder (see Appendix B in DSM-IV-TR for suggested research criteria).

3. Recurrent brief depressive disorder: depressive episodes lasting from 2 days up to 2 weeks, occurring at least once a month for 12 months (not associated with the menstrual cycle) (see Appendix B in DSM-IV-TR for suggested research criteria).

4. Postpsychotic depressive disorder of Schizophrenia: a Major Depressive Episode that occurs during the residual phase of Schizophrenia (see Appendix B in DSM-IV-TR for suggested research criteria).

5. A Major Depressive Episode superimposed on Delusional Disorder, Psychotic Disorder Not Otherwise Specified, or the active phase of Schizophrenia.

6. Situations in which the clinician has concluded that a depressive disorder is present but is unable to determine whether it is primary, due to a general medical condition, or substance induced.

301.13 Cyclothymic Disorder

A. For at least 2 years, the presence of numerous periods with hypomanic symptoms and numerous periods with depressive symptoms that do not meet criteria for a Major Depressive Episode. Note: In children and adolescents, the duration must be at least 1 year.

B. During the above 2-year period (1 year in children and adolescents), the person has not been without the symptoms in Criterion A for more than 2 months at a time.

C. No Major Depressive Episode, Manic Episode, or Mixed Episode has been present during the first 2 years of the disturbance.

Note: After the initial 2 years (1 year in children and adolescents) of Cyclothymic Disorder, there may be superimposed Manic or Mixed Episodes (in which case both Bipolar I Disorder and Cyclothymic Disorder may be diagnosed) or Major Depressive Episodes (in which case both Bipolar II Disorder and Cyclothymic Disorder may be diagnosed).

D. The symptoms in Criterion A are not better accounted for by Schizoaffective Disorder and are not superimposed on Schizophrenia, Schizophreniform Disorder, Delusional Disorder, or Psychotic Disorder Not Otherwise Specified.

E. The symptoms are not due to the direct physiological effects of a substance (e.g., a drug of abuse, a medication) or a general medical condition (e.g., hyperthyroidism).

F. The symptoms cause clinically significant distress or impairment in social, occupational, or other important areas of functioning.

Anxiety Disorders

Because Panic Attacks and Agoraphobia occur in the context of several disorders in this section, criteria sets for a Panic Attack and for Agoraphobia are listed separately at the beginning. They do not, however, have their own diagnostic codes and cannot be diagnosed as separate entities.

Panic Attack

Note: A Panic Attack is not a codable disorder. Code the specific diagnosis in which the Panic Attack occurs (e.g., 300.21 Panic Disorder With Agoraphobia).

A discrete period of intense fear or discomfort, in which four (or more) of the following symptoms developed abruptly and reached a peak within 10 minutes:

(1) palpitations, pounding heart, or accelerated heart rate
(2) sweating
(3) trembling or shaking
(4) sensations of shortness of breath or smothering

(5) feeling of choking
(6) chest pain or discomfort
(7) nausea or abdominal distress
(8) feeling dizzy, unsteady, lightheaded, or faint
(9) derealization (feelings of unreality) or depersonalization (being de-tached from oneself)
(10) fear of losing control or going crazy
(11) fear of dying
(12) paresthesias (numbness or tingling sensations)
(13) chills or hot flushes

Agoraphobia

Note: Agoraphobia is not a codable disorder. Code the specific disorder in which the Agoraphobia occurs (e.g., 300.21 Panic Disorder With Agoraphobia or 300.22 Agoraphobia Without History of Panic Disorder).

A. Anxiety about being in places or situations from which escape might be difficult (or embarrassing) or in which help may not be available in the event of having an unexpected or situationally predisposed Panic Attack or panic-like symptoms. Agoraphobic fears typically involve char-acteristic clusters of situations that include being outside the home alone; being in a crowd or standing in a line; being on a bridge; and traveling in a bus, train, or automobile.
Note: Consider the diagnosis of Specific Phobia if the avoidance is limited to one or only a few specific situations, or Social Phobia if the avoidance is limited to social situations.

B. The situations are avoided (e.g., travel is restricted) or else are en-dured with marked distress or with anxiety about having a Panic At-tack or panic-like symptoms, or require the presence of a companion.

C. The anxiety or phobic avoidance is not better accounted for by an-other mental disorder, such as Social Phobia (e.g., avoidance limited to social situations because of fear of embarrassment), Specific Phobia (e.g., avoidance limited to a single situation like elevators), Obsessive-Compulsive Disorder (e.g., avoidance of dirt in someone with an ob-session about contamination), Posttraumatic Stress Disorder (e.g., avoidance of stimuli associated with a severe stressor), or Separation Anxiety Disorder (e.g., avoidance of leaving home or relatives).

300.01 Panic Disorder Without Agoraphobia
  A. Both (1) and (2):
     (1) recurrent unexpected Panic Attacks
     (2) at least one of the attacks has been followed by 1 month (or more) of one (or more) of the following:
         (a) persistent concern about having additional attacks
         (b) worry about the implications of the attack or its consequences (e.g., losing control, having a heart attack, "going crazy")
         (c) a significant change in behavior related to the attacks
  B. Absence of Agoraphobia.
  C. The Panic Attacks are not due to the direct physiological effects of a substance (e.g., a drug of abuse, a medication) or a general medical condition (e.g., hyperthyroidism).
  D. The Panic Attacks are not better accounted for by another mental disorder, such as Social Phobia (e.g., occurring on exposure to feared social situations), Specific Phobia (e.g., on exposure to a specific phobic situation), Obsessive-Compulsive Disorder (e.g., on exposure to dirt in someone with an obsession about contamination), Posttraumatic Stress Disorder (e.g., in response to stimuli associated with a severe stressor), or Separation Anxiety Disorder (e.g., in response to being away from home or close relatives).

300.21 Panic Disorder With Agoraphobia
  A. Both (1) and (2):
     (1) recurrent unexpected Panic Attacks
     (2) at least one of the attacks has been followed by 1 month (or more) of one (or more) of the following:
         (a) persistent concern about having additional attacks
         (b) worry about the implications of the attack or its consequences (e.g., losing control, having a heart attack, "going crazy")
         (c) a significant change in behavior related to the attacks
  B. The presence of Agoraphobia

C. The Panic Attacks are not due to the direct physiological effects of a substance (e.g., a drug of abuse, a medication) or a general medical condition (e.g., hyperthyroidism).

D. The Panic Attacks are not better accounted for by another mental disorder, such as Social Phobia (e.g., occurring on exposure to feared social situations), Specific Phobia (e.g., on exposure to a specific phobic situation), Obsessive-Compulsive Disorder (e.g., on exposure to dirt in someone with an obsession about contamination), Posttraumatic Stress Disorder (e.g., in response to stimuli associated with a severe stressor), or Separation Anxiety Disorder (e.g., in response to being away from home or close relatives).

300.22 Agoraphobia Without History of Panic Disorder

A. The presence of Agoraphobia related to fear of developing panic-like symptoms (e.g., dizziness or diarrhea).

B. Criteria have never been met for Panic Disorder.

C. The disturbance is not due to the direct physiological effects of a substance (e.g., a drug of abuse, a medication) or a general medical condition.

D. If an associated general medical condition is present, the fear described in Criterion A is clearly in excess of that usually associated with the condition.

300.23 Social Phobia (Social Anxiety Disorder)

A. A marked and persistent fear of one or more social or performance situations in which the person is exposed to unfamiliar people or to possible scrutiny by others. The individual fears that he or she will act in a way (or show anxiety symptoms) that will be humiliating or embarrassing. Note: In children, there must be evidence of the capacity for age-appropriate social relationships with familiar people and the anxiety must occur in peer settings, not just in interactions with adults.

B. Exposure to the feared social situation almost invariably provokes anxiety, which may take the form of a situationally bound or situationally predisposed Panic Attack. Note: In children, the anxiety may be expressed by crying, tantrums, freezing, or shrinking from social situations with unfamiliar people.

C. The person recognizes that the fear is excessive or unreasonable. Note: In children, this feature may be absent.

D. The feared social or performance situations are avoided or else are endured with intense anxiety or distress.

E. The avoidance, anxious anticipation, or distress in the feared social or performance situation(s) interferes significantly with the person's normal routine, occupational (academic) functioning, or social activities or relationships, or there is marked distress about having the phobia.

F. In individuals under age 18 years, the duration is at least 6 months.

G. The fear or avoidance is not due to the direct physiological effects of a substance (e.g., a drug of abuse, a medication) or a general medical condition and is not better accounted for by another mental disorder (e.g., Panic Disorder With or Without Agoraphobia, Separation Anxiety Disorder, Body Dysmorphic Disorder, a Pervasive Developmental Disorder, or Schizoid Personality Disorder).

H. If a general medical condition or another mental disorder is present, the fear in Criterion A is unrelated to it, e.g., the fear is not of Stuttering, trembling in Parkinson's disease, or exhibiting abnormal eating behavior in Anorexia Nervosa or Bulimia Nervosa.

Specify if:

Generalized: if the fears include most social situations (e.g., initiating or maintaining conversations, participating in small groups, dating, speaking to authority figures, attending parties). Note: Also consider the additional diagnosis of Avoidant Personality Disorder.

300.3 Obsessive-Compulsive Disorder

A. Either obsessions or compulsions:

Obsessions as defined by (1), (2), (3), and (4):

(1) recurrent and persistent thoughts, impulses, or images that are experienced, at some time during the disturbance, as intrusive and inappropriate and that cause marked anxiety or distress

(2) the thoughts, impulses, or images are not simply excessive worries about real-life problems

    (3) the person attempts to ignore or suppress such thoughts, impulses, or images, or to neutralize them with some other thought or action

    (4) the person recognizes that the obsessional thoughts, impulses, or images are a product of his or her own mind (not imposed from without as in thought insertion)

Compulsions as defined by (1) and (2):

    (1) repetitive behaviors (e.g., hand washing, ordering, checking) or mental acts (e.g., praying, counting, repeating words silently) that the person feels driven to perform in response to an obsession, or according to rules that must be applied rigidly

    (2) the behaviors or mental acts are aimed at preventing or reducing distress or preventing some dreaded event or situation; however, these behaviors or mental acts either are not connected in a realistic way with what they are designed to neutralize or prevent or are clearly excessive

B. At some point during the course of the disorder, the person has recognized that the obsessions or compulsions are excessive or unreasonable. Note: This does not apply to children.

C. The obsessions or compulsions cause marked distress, are time consuming (take more than 1 hour a day), or significantly interfere with the person's normal routine, occupational (or academic) functioning, or usual social activities or relationships.

D. If another Axis I disorder is present, the content of the obsessions or compulsions is not restricted to it (e.g., preoccupation with food in the presence of an Eating Disorder; hair pulling in the presence of Trichotillomania; concern with appearance in the presence of Body Dysmorphic Disorder; preoccupation with drugs in the presence of a Substance Use Disorder; preoccupation with having a serious illness in the presence of Hypochondriasis; preoccupation with sexual urges or fantasies in the presence of a Paraphilia; or guilty ruminations in the presence of Major Depressive Disorder).

E. The disturbance is not due to the direct physiological effects of a substance (e.g., a drug of abuse, a medication) or a general medical condition.

Specify if:

With Poor Insight: if, for most of the time during the current episode, the person does not recognize that the obsessions and compulsions are excessive or unreasonable

309.81 Posttraumatic Stress Disorder

A. The person has been exposed to a traumatic event in which both of the following were present:

   (1) the person experienced, witnessed, or was confronted with an event or events that involved actual or threatened death or serious injury, or a threat to the physical integrity of self or others

   (2) the person's response involved intense fear, helplessness, or horror. Note: In children, this may be expressed instead by disorganized or agitated behavior

B. The traumatic event is persistently reexperienced in one (or more) of the following ways:

   (1) recurrent and intrusive distressing recollections of the event, including images, thoughts, or perceptions. Note: In young children, repetitive play may occur in which themes or aspects of the trauma are expressed.

   (2) recurrent distressing dreams of the event. Note: In children, there may be frightening dreams without recognizable content.

   (3) acting or feeling as if the traumatic event were recurring (includes a sense of reliving the experience, illusions, hallucinations, and dissociative flashback episodes, including those that occur on awakening or when intoxicated). Note: In young children, trauma-specific reenactment may occur.

   (4) intense psychological distress at exposure to internal or external cues that symbolize or resemble an aspect of the traumatic event.

   (5) physiological reactivity on exposure to internal or external cues that symbolize or resemble an aspect of the traumatic event.

C. Persistent avoidance of stimuli associated with the trauma and numbing of general responsiveness (not present before the trauma), as indicated by three (or more) of the following:

   (1) efforts to avoid thoughts, feelings, or conversations associated with the trauma

(2) efforts to avoid activities, places, or people that arouse recollections of the trauma

(3) inability to recall an important aspect of the trauma

(4) markedly diminished interest or participation in significant activities

(5) feeling of detachment or estrangement from others

(6) restricted range of affect (e.g., unable to have loving feelings)

(7) sense of a foreshortened future (e.g., does not expect to have a career, marriage, children, or a normal life span)

D. Persistent symptoms of increased arousal (not present before the trauma), as indicated by two (or more) of the following:

(1) difficulty falling or staying asleep

(2) irritability or outbursts of anger

(3) difficulty concentrating

(4) hypervigilance

(5) exaggerated startle response

E. Duration of the disturbance (symptoms in Criteria B, C, and D) is more than 1 month.

F. The disturbance causes clinically significant distress or impairment in social, occupational, or other important areas of functioning.

Specify if:

Acute: if duration of symptoms is less than 3 months

Chronic: if duration of symptoms is 3 months or more

Specify if:

With Delayed Onset: if onset of symptoms is at least 6 months after the stressor

308.3 Acute Stress Disorder

A. The person has been exposed to a traumatic event in which both of the following were present:

(1) the person experienced, witnessed, or was confronted with an event or events that involved actual or threatened death or serious injury, or a threat to the physical integrity of self or others

(2) the person's response involved intense fear, helplessness, or horror

B. Either while experiencing or after experiencing the distressing event, the individual has three (or more) of the following dissociative symptoms:

(1) a subjective sense of numbing, detachment, or absence of emotional responsiveness

(2) a reduction in awareness of his or her surroundings (e.g., "being in a daze")

(3) derealization

(4) depersonalization

(5) dissociative amnesia (i.e., inability to recall an important aspect of the trauma)

C. The traumatic event is persistently reexperienced in at least one of the following ways: recurrent images, thoughts, dreams, illusions, flashback episodes, or a sense of reliving the experience; or distress on exposure to reminders of the traumatic event.

D. Marked avoidance of stimuli that arouse recollections of the trauma (e.g., thoughts, feelings, conversations, activities, places, people).

E. Marked symptoms of anxiety or increased arousal (e.g., difficulty sleeping, irritability, poor concentration, hypervigilance, exaggerated startle response, motor restlessness).

F. The disturbance causes clinically significant distress or impairment in social, occupational, or other important areas of functioning or impairs the individual's ability to pursue some necessary task, such as obtaining necessary assistance or mobilizing personal resources by telling family members about the traumatic experience.

G. The disturbance lasts for a minimum of 2 days and a maximum of 4 weeks and occurs within 4 weeks of the traumatic event.

H. The disturbance is not due to the direct physiological effects of a substance (e.g., a drug of abuse, a medication) or a general medical condition, is not better accounted for by Brief Psychotic Disorder, and is not merely an exacerbation of a preexisting Axis I or Axis II disorder.

300.02 Generalized Anxiety Disorder
(Includes Overanxious Disorder of Childhood)

A. Excessive anxiety and worry (apprehensive expectation), occurring more days than not for at least 6 months, about a number of events or activities (such as work or school performance).

B. The person finds it difficult to control the worry.

C. The anxiety and worry are associated with three (or more) of the following six symptoms (with at least some symptoms present for more days than not for the past 6 months). Note: Only one item is required in children.

    (1) restlessness or feeling keyed up or on edge

    (2) being easily fatigued

    (3) difficulty concentrating or mind going blank

    (4) irritability

    (5) muscle tension

    (6) sleep disturbance (difficulty falling or staying asleep, or restless unsatisfying sleep)

D. The focus of the anxiety and worry is not confined to features of an Axis I disorder, e.g., the anxiety or worry is not about having a Panic Attack (as in Panic Disorder), being embarrassed in public (as in Social Phobia), being contaminated (as in Obsessive-Compulsive Disorder), being away from home or close relatives (as in Separation Anxiety Disorder), gaining weight (as in Anorexia Nervosa), having multiple physical complaints (as in Somatization Disorder), or having a serious illness (as in Hypochondriasis), and the anxiety and worry do not occur exclusively during Posttraumatic Stress Disorder.

E. The anxiety, worry, or physical symptoms cause clinically significant distress or impairment in social, occupational, or other important areas of functioning.

F. The disturbance is not due to the direct physiological effects of a substance (e.g., a drug of abuse, a medication) or a general medical condition (e.g., hyperthyroidism) and does not occur exclusively during a Mood Disorder, a Psychotic Disorder, or a Pervasive Developmental Disorder.

293.84 Anxiety Disorder Due to . . . *[Indicate the General Medical Condition]*

    A. Prominent anxiety, Panic Attacks, or obsessions or compulsions predominate in the clinical picture.

B. There is evidence from the history, physical examination, or laboratory findings that the disturbance is the direct physiological consequence of a general medical condition.

C. The disturbance is not better accounted for by another mental disorder (e.g., Adjustment Disorder With Anxiety in which the stressor is a serious general medical condition).

D. The disturbance does not occur exclusively during the course of a delirium.

E. The disturbance causes clinically significant distress or impairment in social, occupational, or other important areas of functioning.

Specify if:

With Generalized Anxiety: if excessive anxiety or worry about a number of events or activities predominates in the clinical presentation

With Panic Attacks: if Panic Attacks predominate in the clinical presentation

With Obsessive-Compulsive Symptoms: if obsessions or compulsions predominate in the clinical presentation

Substance-Induced Anxiety Disorder

A. Prominent anxiety, Panic Attacks, or obsessions or compulsions predominate in the clinical picture.

B. There is evidence from the history, physical examination, or laboratory findings of either (1) or (2):

(1) the symptoms in Criterion A developed during, or within 1 month of, Substance Intoxication or Withdrawal

(2) medication use is etiologically related to the disturbance

C. The disturbance is not better accounted for by an Anxiety Disorder that is not substance induced. Evidence that the symptoms are better accounted for by an Anxiety Disorder that is not substance induced might include the following: the symptoms precede the onset of the substance use (or medication use); the symptoms persist for a substantial period of time (e.g., about a month) after the cessation of acute withdrawal or severe intoxication or are substantially in excess of what would be expected given the type or amount of the substance used or the duration of use; or there is other evidence suggesting the existence of an independent non-substance-induced Anxiety Disorder (e.g., a history of recurrent non-substance-related episodes).

D. The disturbance does not occur exclusively during the course of a delirium.

E. The disturbance causes clinically significant distress or impairment in social, occupational, or other important areas of functioning.

Note: This diagnosis should be made instead of a diagnosis of Substance Intoxication or Substance Withdrawal only when the anxiety symptoms are in excess of those usually associated with the intoxication or withdrawal syndrome and when the anxiety symptoms are sufficiently severe to warrant independent clinical attention.

Specify if:

With Generalized Anxiety: if excessive anxiety or worry about a number of envents or activities predominates in the clinical presentation

With Panic Attacks: if Panic Attacks predominate in the clinical presentation

With Obsessive-Compulsive Symptoms: if obsessions or compulsions predominate in the clinical presentation

With Phobic Symptoms: if phobic symptoms predominate in the clinical presentation

Specify if:

With Onset During Intoxication: if the criteria are met for Intoxication with the substance and the symptoms develop during the intoxication syndrome

With Onset During Withdrawal: if criteria are met for Withdrawal from the substance and the symptoms develop during, or shortly after, a withdrawal syndrome

300.00 Anxiety Disorder Not Otherwise Specified

This category includes disorders with prominent anxiety or phobic avoidance that do not meet criteria for any specific Anxiety Disorder, Adjustment Disorder With Anxiety, or Adjustment Disorder With Mixed Anxiety and Depressed Mood. Examples include

1. Mixed anxiety-depressive disorder: clinically significant symptoms of anxiety and depression, but the criteria are not met for either a specific Mood Disorder or a specific Anxiety Disorder

2. Clinically significant social phobic symptoms that are related to the social impact of having a general medical condition or mental disorder

(e.g., Parkinson's disease, dermatological conditions, Stuttering, Anorexia Nervosa, Body Dysmorphic Disorder)
3. Situations in which the disturbance is severe enough to warrant a diagnosis of an Anxiety Disorder but the individual fails to report enough
symptoms for the full criteria for any specific Anxiety Disorder to have
been met; for example, an individual who reports all of the features of
Panic Disorder Without Agoraphobia except that the Panic Attacks
are all limited-symptom attacks
4. Situations in which the clinician has concluded that an Anxiety Disorder is present but is unable to determine whether it is primary, due to
a general medical condition, or substance induced

Adjustment Disorders

Adjustment Disorders

A. The development of emotional or behavioral symptoms in response
to an identifiable stressor(s) occurring within 3 months of the onset of
the stressor(s).
B. These symptoms or behaviors are clinically significant as evidenced by
either of the following:
   (1) marked distress that is in excess of what would be expected from
   exposure to the stressor
   (2) significant impairment in social or occupational (academic) functioning
C. The stress-related disturbance does not meet the criteria for another
specific Axis I disorder and is not merely an exacerbation of a preexisting Axis I or Axis II disorder.
D. The symptoms do not represent Bereavement.
E. Once the stressor (or its consequences) has terminated, the symptoms
do not persist for more than an additional 6 months.

Specify if:

Acute: if the disturbance lasts less than 6 months

Chronic: if the disturbance lasts for 6 months or longer. By definition, symptoms
cannot persist for more than 6 months after the termination of the stressor or its
consequences. The Chronic specifier therefore applies when the duration of the
disturbance is longer than 6 months in response to a chronic stressor or to a

stressor that has enduring consequences.

Adjustment Disorders are coded based on the subtype, which is selected according to the predominant symptoms. The specific stressor(s) can be specified on Axis IV.

309.0 With Depressed Mood: when the predominant manifestations are symptoms such as depressed mood, tearfulness, or feelings of hopelessness

309.24 With Anxiety: when the predominant manifestations are symptoms such as nervousness, worry, or jitteriness, or, in children, fears of separation from major attachment figures

309.28 With Mixed Anxiety and Depressed Mood: when the predominant manifestation is a combination of depression and anxiety

309.3 With Disturbance of Conduct: when the predominant manifestation is a disturbance in conduct in which there is violation of the rights of others or of major age-appropriate societal norms and rules (e.g., truancy, vandalism, reckless driving, fighting, defaulting on legal responsibilities)

309.4 With Mixed Disturbance of Emotions and Conduct: when the predominant manifestations are both emotional symptoms (e.g., depression, anxiety) and a disturbance of conduct (see above subtype)

309.9 Unspecified: for maladaptive reactions (e.g., physical complaints, social withdrawal, or work or academic inhibition) to stressors that are not classifiable as one of the specific subtypes of Adjustment Disorder

Guide to Medications

Most of these medications are mentioned in *Toxic Stress* and are among the most commonly prescribed for depression, anxiety and certain other conditions. There are many other medications on the market, and we are hopeful about new medications that are working their way through the federal drug approval process.

If you feel you need to "jumpstart" your recovery from toxic stress, talk to your doctor about medication. Psychologists in most states, including Florida, are not licensed to prescribe medicine, but we work closely with our patients' psychiatrists and primary care physicians to track the effectiveness and side effects of medications.

Antidepressants

SSRIs (selective serotonin re-uptake inhibitors)

These are often prescribed for depression, and some have antianxiety qualities, as well. Some are available in time-release formulas that are helpful to people who have difficulty taking medication at regular intervals through the day. Controlled release and extended release are sometimes noted as CR or XR, respectively, after the medication name; SR indicates standard release. SSRI medications cause the brain to retain serotonin, which improves mood.

SSRIs

Brand Name	Generic Name
Celexa™	citalopram
Effexor®	venlafaxine
Lexapro™	escitalopram oxalate
Luvox®	fluoxetine
Paxil®	paroxetine
Prozac®	fluoxetine hydrochloride
Remeron®	mirtazapine
Serzone®	nefazodone
Zoloft®	sertraline

Tricyclic Antidepressants

Brand Name	Generic Name
Adapin®	doxepin
Asendin®	amoxapine
Elavil®	amitriptyline
Norpramin®	desipramine
Pamelor®	nortriptyline
Tofranil®	imipramine

MAO (monoamine oxidase) inhibitors

Brand Name	Generic Name
Nardil®	phenelzine
Parnate®	tranylcypromine

Other Antidepressants

Also prescribed for depression is bupropion in the aminoketone class of medications. It is also a non-nicotine aid to smoking cessation with fewer negative effects on sexual performance than some other antidepressants.

Brand Name	Generic Name
Wellbutrin®	bupropion

Antianxiety Medications

SSRIs listed under antidepressants are also prescribed for certain anxiety diagnoses.

Benzodiazepines

Brand Name	Generic Name
Ativan®	lorazepam
Klonopin®	clonazepam
Valium®	diazepam
Xanax®	alprazolam

Other Antianxiety Medications

Brand Name	Generic Name
BuSpar®	buspirone

Medications Often Prescribed to Improve Sleep

Brand Name	Generic Name
Ambien®	zolpidem
Restoril®	emazepam
Sonata®	zaleplon

Also Benadryl®, over-the-counter

New Atypical Antipsychotic Medications

Brand Name	Generic Name
Abilify™	aripiprazole
Geodon®	ziprasidone
Seroquel™	quetiapine fumarate

ADHD Medications

These are commonly prescribed medications for Attention Deficit Hyperactivity Disorder. Some come in extended release forms.

Brand Name	Generic Name
Strattera®	atomoxetine
Ritalin®	methylphenidate
Adderall®	amphetamine mixed salts
Concerta®	methylphenidate

Over-the-Counter "Supplements"

Saint-John's-wort
SAM-e

Bibliotherapy

I have always recommended bibliotherapy for my patients. At the top of the list now will be *Toxic Stress: 7 Steps to Recovery*. Still, the books here offer deeper insights into particular issues, and I hope you will find them helpful.

Anger Management

Borcherdt, B. (2000). *You Can Control Your Anger! 21 Ways To Do It*. Sarasota, FL: Professional Resource Exchange.

Ellis, A. (1977). *Anger: How to Live With and Without It*. Secaucus, NJ: Citadel Press.

Lerner, H. (1985). *The Dance of Anger: A Woman's Guide to Changing the Patterns of Intimate Relationships*. New York: Harper Perennial.

McKay, M., P. Rogers, and J. McKay (1989). *When Anger Hurts*. Oakland, CA: New Harbinger.

Rubin, T. I. (1969). *The Angry Book*. New York: Macmillan.

Tavris, C. (1989). *Anger: The Misunderstood Emotion*. New York: Touchstone Books.

Williams, R., and V. Williams (1989). *Anger Kills*. New York: HarperCollins.

Anxiety

Benson, H. (1975). *The Relaxation Response*. New York: William Morrow.

Bernstein, D., and T. Borkovec (1973). *Progressive Relaxation Training*. Champaign, IL: Research Press.

Carnegie, D. (1984). *How to Stop Worrying and Start Living.* New York: Simon & Schuster.

Davis, M., E. Eshelman, and M. McKay (1988). *The Relaxation and Stress Reduction Workbook.* Oakland, CA: New Harbinger.

DeRosis, H. (1979). *Women and Anxiety.* New York: Delacorte Press.

Ellis, A. (1998). *A Guide to Rational Living.* North Hollywood, CA: Wilshire Book Co.

Ellis, A. (1998). *How to Control Your Anxiety Before It Controls You.* New York: Citadel Press.

Hauck, P. (1975). *Overcoming Worry and Fear.* Philadelphia: Westminster Press.

Jeffers, S. (1987). *Feel the Fear and Do It Anyway.* San Diego: Harcourt Brace Jovanovich.

Marks, I. (1980). *Living with Fear: Understanding and Coping with Anxiety.* New York: McGraw-Hill.

Weekes, C. (1969). *Hope and Help for Your Nerves.* New York: Signet.

Weekes, C. (1972). *Peace From Nervous Suffering.* New York: Bantam Books.

Assertiveness Training

Albert, K., and M. Emmons (1990). *Your Perfect Right.* San Luis Obispo, CA: Impact.

Longe, A., and P. Jakubowski (1976). *Responsible Assertive Behavior.* Champaign, IL: Research Press.

Phelps, S., and N. Austin (1987). *The Assertive Woman.* San Luis Obispo, CA: Impact.

Smith, M. (1985). *When I Say No I Feel Guilty.* New York: Bantam Books.

Attention Deficit Disorder

Conners, C. K., and Juliet Jett (1999). *Attention Deficit Hyperactivity Disorder.* Kansas City, MO: Compact Clinicals.

Hallowell, E., and J. Ratey (1994). *Driven to Distraction.* New York: Simon & Schuster.

Weis, Lynn. (1994). *The Attention Deficit Disorder in Adults Workbook.* Dallas: Taylor Publishing.

Wender, P. (1987). *The Hyperactive Child, Adolescent and Adult.* New York: Oxford.

Counseling and Psychotherapy

Ellis, A. (1979). *Reason and Emotion in Psychotherapy.* Secaucus, NJ: The Citadel Press.

Horon, J. (1979). *Counseling for Effective Decision Making.* Belmont, CA: Wadsworth Publishing Co.

Lazarus, A. (1971). *Behavior Therapy and Beyond.* New York: McGraw Hill.

Mahoney, M. (1980). *Psychotherapy Process.* New York: Plenum Press.

Depression

Burns, D. (1980). *Feeling Good: The New Mood Therapy.* New York: Signet.

Burns, D. (1989). *The Feeling Good Handbook.* New York: Plume.

Butler, P. (1991). *Talking to Yourself: Learning the Language of Self Affirmation.* New York: Stein and Day.

DePaulo, J. R., and K. R. Ablow (1995). *How to Cope with Depression.* New York: McGraw-Hill.

Greist, J., and J. Jefferson (1984). *Depression and Its Treatment.* Washington, DC: American Psychiatric Press.

Hallinan, P. K. (1976). *One Day at a Time.* Minneapolis: CompCare.

Lewinsohn, P. M. (1986). *Control Your Depression.* New York: Prentice Hall Press.

Preston, J. (2001). *Lift Your Mood Now.* Oakland, CA: New Harbinger.

Preston, J. (1996). *You Can Beat Depression.* San Luis Obispo, CA: Import Publications.

Seligman, M. (1990). *Learned Optimism: The Skill to Conquer Life's Obstacles, Large and Small.* New York: Pocket Books.

Family Conflict

Bradshaw, J. (1988). *On the Family.* Deerfield Beach, FL: Health Communications, Inc.

Drews, T. R. (1980). *Getting Them Sober: A Guide for Those Living with Alcoholism.* South Plainfield, NJ: Bridge Publishing.

Fassler, D., M. Lash, and S. Ivers (1988). *Changing Families.* Burlington, VT: Waterfront Books.

Ginott, H. (1969). *Between Parent and Child.* New York: Macmillan.

Ginott, H. (1969). *Between Parent and Teenager.* New York: Macmillan.

Glenn, S., and J. Nelsen (1989). *Raising Self-Reliant Children in a Self Indulgent World.* Rocklin, CA: Prima.

Guerney, Louise F. (1980). *Parenting: A Skills Training Manual.* Bethesda, MD: National Institute of Relationship Enhancement.

Grief

Colgrone, M., H. Bloomfield, and P. McWilliams (1991). *How to Survive the Loss of a Love.* Los Angeles: Prelude Press.

Studacher, C. (1987). *Beyond Grief: A Guide for Recovering from the Death of a Loved One.* Oakland, CA: Harbinger Publications.

Panic Disorder and Phobias

Gold, M. (1988). *The Good News About Panic, Anxiety, and Phobias.* New York: Villard/Random House.

Ross, J. (1994). *Triumph over Fear.* New York: Bantam Books.

Swede, S., and S. Jaffe (1987). *The Panic Attack Recovery Book.* New York: New American Library.

Wilson, R. (1986). *Don't Panic: Taking Control of Anxiety Attacks.* New York: Harper & Row.

Relationship Issues

Abrahms-Spring, J. (1996). *After the Affair.* New York: HarperCollins.

Bach, G., and P. Wyden (1976). *The Intimate Enemy: How to Fight Fair in Love and Marriage.* New York: Avon Books.

Beck, A. (1968). *Love Is Never Enough.* New York: Harper & Row Publications.

Burns, D. (1985). *Intimate Connections.* New York: Signet Publication.

Buscaglia, L. (1982). *Living, Loving and Learning.* New York: Ballantine Books.

Colgrove, M., H. Bloomfield, and P. McWilliams (1991). *How to Survive the Loss of a Love.* Los Angeles: Prelude Press.

Dattilio, F., and C. Padesky (1990). *Cognitive Therapy with Couples.* Sarasota, FL: Professional Resource Exchange.

Fisher, B. (1981). *ReBuilding: When Your Relationship Ends.* San Luis Obispo, CA: Impact.

Fromm, E. (1956). *The Art of Loving.* New York: Harper & Row.

Gorski, T. (1993). *Getting Love Right: Learning the Choices of Healthy Intimacy.* New York: Simon & Schuster.

Gottman, J., C. Notarius, J. Gonso, and H. Markman (1976). *A Couple's Guide to Communication.* Champaign, IL: Research Press.

Gray, J. (1993). *Men and Women and Relationships: Making Peace with the Opposite Sex.* Hillsboro, OR: Beyond Words.

Gray, J. (1992). *Men Are from Mars, Women Are from Venus.* New York: HarperCollins.

Harley, W. (1994). *His Needs, Her Needs: Building an Affair-Proof Marriage.* Grand Rapids, MI: Revill.

Hendrix, H. (1988). *Getting the Love You Want.* New York: Harper Perennial.

Kaplan, B. (1999). *Soul Dating to Soul Mating.* New York: Perigee.

Keyes, K. (1979). *A Conscious Person's Guide to Relationships.* Coos Bay, OR: Cornucopia Books.

Lerner, H. (1989). *The Dance of Intimacy.* New York: Harper & Row Publishing.

McGraw, P. (2000). *Relationship Rescue.* New York: Hyperion.

Paul, J., and M. Paul (1983). *Do I Have To Give Up Me To Be Loved By You?* Minneapolis: CompCare Publishers.

Whitfield, C. (1993). *Boundaries and Relationships.* Deerfield Beach, FL: Health Communication, Inc.

Self-Esteem

Branden, N. (1969). *The Psychology of Self-Esteem.* New York: Bantam Books.

Branden, N. (1994). *The Six Pillars of Self-Esteem.* New York: Bantam Books.

Burns, D. (1993). *Ten Days to Self Esteem!* New York: William Morrow.

Marotta, P. (1999). *Power and Wisdom: The New Path for Women.* Plantation, FL: Women of Wisdom, Inc.

McGraw, P. (2001). *Self Matters: Creating Your Life from the Inside Out.* New York, Simon & Schuster Source.

McKay, M., and P. Fanning (1987). *Self-Esteem.* Oakland, CA: New Harbinger.

Phillips, G. (1981). *Help for Shy People.* New York: Dorset Press.

Shapiro, L. (1993). *Building Blocks of Self Esteem.* King of Prussia, PA: Center for Applied Psychology.

Zimbardo, P. (1987). *Shyness: What It Is and What to Do About It.* Reading, MA: Addison-Wesley.

Sexual Dysfunction

Barbach, L. (1982). *For Each Other: Sharing Sexual Intimacy.* New York: Doubleday.

Comfort, A. (1991). *The New Joy of Sex.* New York: Crown.

Corn, L. (2001). *The Great American Sex Diet.* New York: Harper Collins.

Heiman, J., and J. LoPiccolo (1988). *Becoming Orgasmic: A Sexual Growth Program for Women.* New York: Prentice-Hall.

Masters, W., and V. Johnson (1974). *The Pleasure Bond: A New Look at Sexuality and Commitment.* Boston: Little Brown.

McCarthy, B., and E. McCarthy (1984). *Sexual Awareness.* New York: Carroll & Graft.

Zilbergeld, B. (1992). *The New Male Sexuality.* New York: Bantam Books.

Sleep Disorder

Dotto, L. (1990). *Losing Sleep: How Your Sleeping Habits Affect Your Life.* New York: William Morrow.

Hewish, J. (1985). *Relaxation.* Chicago: NTC Publishing Group.

Sweeney, D. (1989). *Overcoming Insomnia: A Medical Program for Problem Sleepers.* New York: G.P. Putnam's Sons.

Spirituality

Chopra, D. (1993). *Ageless Body Timeless Mind.* New York: Harmony Books.

Chopra, D. (2001). *The Deeper Wound, Recovering the Soul from Fear and Suffering.* New York: Harmony Books.

Frankel, V. (1959). *Man's Search for Meaning.* New York: Simon & Schuster.

Peck, M. S. (1978). *The Road Less Traveled.* New York: Simon & Schuster.

Weiss, B. (2000). *Messages From The Master Tapping into the Power of Love.* New York: Warner Books.

Stress Management

Benson, H., and E. Stuart (1992). *The Wellness Book: The Comprehensive Guide to Maintaining Health and Treating Stress Related Illness.* New York: Birch Lane Press.

Charlesworth, E., and R. Nathon (1982). *Stress Management.* New York: Ballantine Books.

Kirsta, A. (1986). *The Book of Stress Survival*. New York: Simon & Schuster.

Lazarus, J. (2000). *Stress Relief and Relaxation Techniques*. Lincolnwood, IL: Keats Publishing.

Sapolsky, R. (1998). *Why Zebras Don't Get Ulcers*. New York: W.H. Freeman.

Weight Control

Agatston, A. (2003). *The South Beach Diet*. New York: Rodale Press.

Atkins, R. (1999). *Dr. Atkins' New Diet Revolution*. New York: Avon Books.

Brown, M., and J. Robinson (2002). *When Your Body Gets the Blues*. New York: Berkley Books.

Mahoney. M, and K. Mahoney (1976). *Permanent Weight Control*. New York: Norton & Company.

Miller, P. (1983). *The Hilton Head Metabolism Diet*. New York: Warner Books.

Peeke, P. (2000). *Fight Fat After Forty*. New York: Penguin Books.

Sears, B. (1997). *The Zone: Revolutionary Life Plan to Put Your Body in Balance for Permanent Weight Loss*. New York: HarperCollins.

Steward, H. Leighton, et al. (2003). *The New Sugar Busters*. New York: Ballantine.

Wurtman, J. (1996). *The Serotonin Solution*. New York: Fawcett Columbine.

Guide to Strategies and Techniques

Index